To Betty

CHASING SHADOWS

Warm regards to

Daryl May

good friends

signature

DocUmeant *Publishing*
244 5th Avenue
Suite G-200
NY, NY 10001
646-233-4366
www.DocUmeantPublishing.com

Published by
DocUmeant Publishing
244 5th Avenue, Suite G-200
NY, NY 10001

646-233-4366

Disclaimer: While I have used real names to acknowledge the many wonderful people included in this book, I have opted to change the names of a few people who might otherwise be less than delighted to find themselves mentioned and those who are no longer with us.

Library of Congress Control Number: 2016940700

ISBN13: 978-1-937801-66-3 (14.97)
ISBN10: 1937801667

Dedication

I wish to dedicate this book to my beautiful wife Brenda, who has, without question or doubt, supported and encouraged me in all my dreams and endeavors, to my daughter Wendy-Doodle, whose kindness and sense of humor surpasses all others, to my stepson Robert Kildoo, to my grandkids ("Grandboogers"): Mariah Pelley, Garrett Pelley, Morgan Scott May, Olivia Rose Pelley, and Carly Rose May, "gooderns all" and especially to my wonderful daughter Perri Jo May-Pelley, who embodied courage, faith, and love during her long, courageous battle with cancer. I miss and think of her every day . . . and will to my final breath.

Special Dedication

The book is also dedicated to my brother Gary A. May, formerly with Illinois' Champaign County Sheriff's Office and the Pinellas County Sheriff's Office (Ret.), my son Scott A. May, detective with the Pinellas County Sheriff's Office and the United States Army Reserve, and to the late Sheriff Don Genung, his wife Florence, and the men and women who served with honor and distinction with the Pinellas County Sheriff's Office during my tenure with that excellent organization.

Acknowledgments

I would like to recognize the following people, whose help, encouragement, and support have been invaluable. First and foremost, a big thanks to Enola Jane Lewis Moon, for providing suggestions and directions, making me look much better with my grammar and prose and to my longtime friend George Miller for his artwork.

A very special thanks for encouragement and technical advice goes to my stepson Robert Kildoo, ("The Guru"), professional photographer, and for the book cover photo and his perpetual patience for fine tuning and keeping my PC up and running, and to Pastor Bruce Little (PCSO, FBI, Ret.), Leroy Kelly (PPPD, CPD, PCSO, PCPAO, IRCPAO, Ret.), Maj. Gen. Sandy "The Stealth Guy" Sharpe (USAF, Ret.), the late James "Jim" Pochurek (Lt. Col., USAF, Ret.), Patricia Pochurek (Journalist), and last but definitely not least, Judge Joe Donahey (Ret.), who has read everything I've written and offered advice and encouragement.

A big thank you goes to my good friends Dr. Pete "Cuz" May, Jim Moore (SO, FBI, GTE, Ret.), Maj. Frank Holloway (PCSO, Ret.), Warren King (SO, Ret.), Mike Sharpe (SO Ret.), and Skip Dequire. Also, thanks to Charlotte Dillon, Jan Gidley, and Derek Burnett, the Reader's Digest guy. Because of these friends, I turned the corner and became serious about writing *Chasing Shadows.*

A Memoir

"It only takes three things to be a writer.
First, you got to have something to say.
Secondly, you got to have the ability to say it, and
Thirdly, you got to have the courage to say it all."
—Maya Angelou

Contents

DEDICATION iii

SPECIAL DEDICATION iii

ACKNOWLEDGMENTS v

PART I

The Shoot 1

"Does Your Husband Have a Gun?" 14

"I Ain't Going No Wheres With You, Deputy." 37

Learning the Ropes 47

The Judge & The Rooster 59

Roy M. Speer, Attorney 65

Sheriff Don Genung 69

The Marble 79

Bruce Little 89

"Little Red Riding Hooker" 96

Perri 106

PART II

George Alden May 113

"The Sirens' Call" 114

Comedy: The Big Stick 130

Sea Wake 139

"On The Prowl with Caroline Kennedy" 148

PART III

Hat Tricks 157

Sacred Moment 170

The Song Writer 178

Up Yours* 200

ADDENDUM 207

ABOUT THE AUTHOR .213

ALSO AVAILABLE 215

Part I

"If you can imagine it, it will happen.
Dreams and goals don't always come easy.
Finding success and good fortune
Is sometimes like chasing shadows."
—Grandfather John Erit Charles May
  (b.1874-d.1950)

CHAPTER ONE

The Shoot

"You sleep safe in your beds because
Rough men stand ready in the night to visit
Violence on those who would do you harm."
—George Orwell

IT IS SAID FLORIDA weather is made up mostly of nine months of perpetual spring, and three months of intolerable hell. Those summer months, interrupted by hurricanes, are mostly sweltering and sticky.

Air conditioning for county vehicles in the 1960s consisted of what we called 4-and-60. Meaning you rolled down all four windows and drove 60 miles an hour. I had spent the first years of my life dealing with nasty and prolonged Illinois winters and I was glad to now live in Clearwater. I was young and skinny and could easily handle the subtropical heat. It was an agreeable trade-off.

For the better part of the afternoon and evening I'd been staking out a fugitive's house in a remote agriculture area between Ozona and Tarpon Springs. The mosquitoes were humming-bird size, big enough to carry wing tanks.

Trying to catch up with Elwood "Keek" Lee, a six foot 3-plus black guy, born and raised in Pinellas County hadn't been easy. There was a felony warrant for his arrest and he had foolishly elected not to appear before Pinellas Circuit Judge B. J. Driver on a charge of aggravated assault. Given the choices, maybe I too would have taken a hike instead of going before Driver.

For the umpteenth time Keek was in trouble for drinking copious amounts of shine—stuff the locals called low bush lightening—and this time he had brandished a grapefruit knife, a long and narrow pocket blade, to settle a spat. He was an angry man. Not all together congenial when sober, but after throwing back a few, he could be downright unpleasant. Some deputies had learned that. You never knew if things might go south when dealing with the man. A lot of deputies knew that, too. A *"unanimous"* female caller—probably his mama—informed the office that morning saying Keek would most likely show up at the house he occupied with his common law wife. He wanted to say goodbye to Anita and their two little girls before "hot-footing" it north, probably to Atlanta. The caller said, "He say, he ain't goin' back to no jail, no way . . . no how!"

||||||||||||||||||||||||||||||||||||||||||||||||||||||||||||||||||||||||
"I shoved the short steel barrel hard against that soft spot just below his right rib cage and lit one off. There was a violent, lightning quick impact. The weapon going off between two bodies—two struggling masses of muscle, blood, and bone— carried a deadly consequence."

||||||||||||||||||||||||||||||||||||||||||||||||||||||||||||||||||||||||

I got to know Keek Lee when he was a promising high school footballer, before his daddy pulled him out of school to work his mullet boat. Keek could drill a football with the speed of a .45 caliber hollow point or fling a seven foot cast net farther than crusty Whit Whitaker, known locally as the Cast Net King. Whitaker bragged that all his life he'd "done battle with mullet in the harbor and angry men in juke joints."

Keek's reluctance to go before Driver was understandable. The former World War Two combat Marine was recognized as a tough adjudicator. Coming home from the war he continued to wear a G.I. burr cut and dictate whether lawyers appearing before him could wear facial hair.

Snowbirds were welcomed with open arms during winters, but come Easter, they were expected to pay up, get the hell outta Dodge and get back on the other side of the Mason-Dixon Line. Segregation lingered when I came to town, and there remained a definite cultural distinction between blacks and whites, real and imagined. Old timers spoke fondly of days when the Klan met secretly in Palm Harbor. Crosses got fired up with regularity on weekends at the north end of the county. Inside the courthouse, signs clearly marked drinking fountains for Whites and for Colored. "Whites Only" restrooms were conveniently located on the main floor. But Blacks were forced to take two flights of stairs to the basement. Just as portrayed in Harper Lee's novel *To Kill A Mocking Bird*, blacks sat in the courtroom balcony except, of course, when they were defendants.

This was all very new to me. Born and raised in Potomac, a small farm community near Danville, IL, I could probably count on one hand the times I'd had an exchange or even been close to a black person. My high school had 97 students—all white.

In 1957, I had only recently arrived in Florida and witnessed racial intolerance for the first time at the Capitol Theater in downtown Clearwater. I went to see *Island In The Sun*, a movie that opened with the voice of Harry Belafonte, an American songwriter, actor, and social activist, singing the title song over aerial views of a fictitious Caribbean island. The film's plot depicted an interracial romance between Belafonte and Joan Fontaine, a white British-American actress. By today's standards the affair wasn't particularly graphic or in-your-face.

I doubt anyone as far south as Clearwater knew the movie had been banned in Memphis, TN, because of its "frank depiction of miscegenation, an offense to moral standards and no good for Whites or Negroes." Fontaine would receive a flood of hate mail because of her character's desire for an interracial romance with the character played by Belafonte, an island lawyer. The flick was causing a great deal of controversy as far north as Minneapolis, MN. In New Orleans, the American Legion had launched a campaign to halt the film's screening on the grounds that it "contributes to the Communist Party's aim of creating friction between the races."

I was a big fan of Belafonte and owned a couple of his record albums. Being young—and relatively oblivious to racism—I went to the Saturday afternoon premier. There was a full house. The movie had no sooner gotten underway before people, seeing where the yarn was headed, began stomping out. Many didn't bother leaving via the lobby entrance but noisily hit the exits on both sides of the stage, sending intermittent blasts of sunlight into the darkened auditorium.

I am not suggesting Judge Billy Joe Driver, born white in Mayo, Florida, was prejudiced or a racist but he was tutored in life and law by old John U. Bird, the "high judge" in the early 1950s who administered over all felony cases in Pinellas County. Bird, also born and bred in the Deep South, adhered to deep-rooted values that clung to the principles and concepts of the Confederacy. Authoritative and obese, Bird might have easily played Orson Welles' part of Big Daddy in the 1958 movie *The Long Hot Summer*. He addressed black attorneys by their first names and made it clear he didn't want them on his home property at any time, day or night, for any reason. Nevertheless, he was sometimes described as considerate of "those people" that came before him in court because he understood and sometimes sympathized with their plight in what was then the "Jim Crow" South.

Known in law enforcement circles as the hanging judge, Driver had given me an unwarranted butt-chewing for an infraction I had not committed. I was obliged to stand before him in his crowded courtroom, in uniform, hat in hand, and take his humiliating, long-winded bullshit. He cared little about who suffered degradation so long as he demonstrated judicial authority over lawyers, jurors, and courtroom spectators. I sensed no humor in the man on or off the bench.

Even so, there were stories known only to a few. Among Driver's personal belongings was a Purple Heart. Another judge told me that in September 4, 1944, Driver was a young Marine with an invasion force that shipped out from Pavuvu, just north of Guadalcanal, and sailed 2,100 miles across the Pacific to the island of Peleliu, present-day Palau. The small coral atoll was occupied and heavily fortified by 11,000 Japanese. Subsequently, during a heavy and deadly push by the enemy, Driver, in a shallow foxhole, stood up deliberately in the 115-degree heat. As machine gun fire raked the sand around him, he held his fire for a Japanese tank to move-in closer. When the moment was right, he triggered his bazooka and, with a fiery blast, stopped the tank dead in its tracks. Still targeted by enemy gun fire, Driver reloaded and took-out a second enemy tank. He continued standing in a rain of automatic weapons fire, reloaded again and knocked out a third tank. For this action, B.J. Driver, who saw 90–percent of his company wiped out, came home with the Navy Cross, a Purple Heart, and two presidential unit citations. He was credited with single-handedly stopping a Japanese assault.

So, there I was parked in the evening shadows, keeping a watchful eye on Keek Lee's shanty. The light sprinkles had stopped. The air was damp and the evening had cooled off some. Everything was muffled and subdued. By ten-thirty I'd concluded my guy was a no-show and decided to go home. For all I knew, during the inter-mittent rains, Keek had parked somewhere in an orange grove, and slipped in the back way. He'd probably already come and gone, flown the coop. I got on the horn, called the uniform car working that zone to let him know I was going home.

If and when I, or any other guy carrying the tin (badge), caught up with Keek, he'd have hell-to-pay. Facing Driver would not be pleasant. If his sentence was less than a year it would be spent in the county jail and close to home. But, if Driver had a burr up his butt Keek would find himself working on a chain gang chopping weeds along some South Florida blacktop. But, he knew all that. This wasn't his first barbeque.

My day had started out—like most other days—with a handful of warrants, replevins, and other court papers. I was ending the shift with the same stack. Serving papers was a numbers game and I was becoming acclimated to it, marking time to get through the shift. The sheriff had decided, without discussion, that my nearly four years in the vice squad were enough. He was fond of saying that any deputy spending more than three years in vice began suspecting everyone including his mother-in-law and the neighbor's dog. But good vice cops were hard to come by. Not everyone was interested or capable of doing that kind of work. It required a quick mind, the ability to think on your feet, to deal with stressful situations and have an uncanny knack for lying. In the song *The American Soldier*, Toby Keith sings, "I was damn good under pressure." I'd like to think I and the other vice guys fit in that category.

I was thinking long and hard about my unexpected and unwanted transfer from vice. Now, instead of busting dopers, keeping tabs on the Palm Harbor Klan, and harassing the Tampa Mafia, I was driving around serving subpoenas, divorce papers, and an occasional arrest warrant. Individual stacks of important looking papers, bound with heavy red rubber bands, were organized and neatly packed in shallow cardboard boxes on the front seat of this straight-shift piece of rolling junk called a Ford. It was easy to figure out how long a guy had worked in Civil and Warrants (C&W) by the number of cardboard boxes cluttering the back seat and the collection of moldy rubber bands hanging on the gear shift.

The division was made up of older men content with closing out their careers on a low note. It was supposed to be a relatively safe eight-to-fiver. But before I'd come on the job two old timers had shot it out with a deranged retiree.

A psychiatrist had arranged for the deputies to meet him at a private residence to transport a schizophrenic to the State Hospital at Chattahoochee, up in the panhandle. Brandishing a loaded 7 mm German Lugar, the patient ambushed the lawmen and killed the doctor. The sicko died a bloody naked heap in the shootout on the expansive manicured lawn of his Belleair mansion.

Both deputies accepted early retirement after lengthy recupera-
tions caused by multiple gunshot wounds.

But, all in all, the job was a cherry gig for the uninspired. As long
as the paperwork was processed in a timely manner, little was said
about how a deputy spent his workday. Younger guys transferred to
the unit had likely screwed up politically or otherwise displeased a
major or captain. In my case, the sheriff thought I needed a break
from Vice & Intelligence and had no place else to put me.

The single thing that made the mundane job sufferable was my
captain. Ella Léon, an older and classy Jewish lady, who treated me
like a son. She understood my vexation with the transfer and realized that after working Mafia dogfights and red whisky raids that
it wasn't an easy transition for me; a young, street wise investigator
with a lot of experience under my belt, now coping with the petty
crap of serving papers.

But, what the heck, I was in a pretty good mood. I'd been thinking about packing it in anyhow. After seven years, I'd had about
as much fun and excitement that law enforcement could offer. I'd
busted more than my share of bad asses and seen enough blood
and gore to last three lifetimes. I'd experienced some close calls,
and had a ton of laughs.

There had been a slew of interesting moments. I'd been handpicked
to work a first line security detail for President Jack Kennedy in
Tampa, four days before he was murdered in Dallas. I was close
enough to the most powerful man in the world to feel his energy.
I smelled the cigar on his jacket and sensed his aura. There were
other events. More than once I'd helped to physically lift a squirrely
Claude Kirk, campaigning for governor, from his private plane
because he was too hammered to navigate a straight line. Later, I
guarded him when he visited Pinellas County as governor. There
were memorable stints working security details and chatting
with icons such as Chet Atkins, Arnold Palmer, Bob Hope, Ed
McMahon, and Frank Sinatra. Perhaps all that exposure to celebrity
was rubbing off on me. Maybe I was getting a little star struck and

wanted a piece of that kind of action, not yet understanding there was something creative and imaginative in me trying to break out. The urge had been there a long time, an urge for expression. I just didn't know how to get it done, yet. Two years of secretly studying voice while working as a meat cutter with the Quick Check-Winn Dixie grocery chain proved something. I kept it a secret from the macho yo-yos on the job that I was spending my one day off humming and me-meing the musical scale until my eyes watered and my nose dripped.

I had a strong hankering to play the guitar and try my hand at song writing. I knew I had an excellent gimmick that would set me apart from the regular run-of-the-mill bar pickers. I was a deputy sheriff that could flat sing. That made me different from the rest of the mob out there playing bar gigs. I knew I could write some good stuff if I had the time and practice. I could think of little else. My granddad's words kept coming back to me, something about chasing shadows, working hard to make dreams come true.

One of the considerations that kept me from pulling the plug then and there was knowing if I'd hang in another three years I'd eventually have some kind of retirement check coming my way, albeit small. For a married guy with three kids it was something that needed serious thought.

Another thing; how the heck did one get from Point A to Point B? I mean, how do you go about making the transition, leaving a full-time, established 8-to-5 job, and then making ends meet financially while getting established as an entertainer? How long would it take? Who could give me that kind of advice? The subject was not covered in my little corn-town high school . . . or sociology studies at St. Pete Junior College.

I had a lot of my dad in me. He had been his own man all his life. He was a skilled cabinetmaker by trade but in his youth had worked a lot of menial jobs. During the depression he'd cut wood for fifty cents a day just to put bread on the table. He'd been a meat cutter for a while. During World War II he was a firefighter at a crash station at Chanute Air Base in Rantoul, Illinois. To a little kid, like me, the job sounded exciting. He'd come home and tell how he held onto the back of a screaming fire truck, getting to a B-25 Mitchell bomber with an engine on fire or chasing a Boeing B-17 Flying Fortress skidding off a rain soaked runway.

Perhaps I should have been content. Law enforcement beat the "going-nowhere job" I gave up as assistant manager in a grocery chain. I had been floundering in my quest for the American dream. Now I had a great loving family, a new house with a mortgage, and was making tolerable payments on a used Chevy. This job was respectable with excellent benefits. Chances of making sergeant looked promising and would bring my salary up to about seven grand a year which would then guarantee that I'd be stuck in that one work place for the next 25 or 30 years.

But I was having novel thoughts that balmy night. A week or so earlier, during a conversation with another guitar player, a Pasco deputy, he mentioned that country legend Johnny Cash and his wife June Carter-Cash owned a house up on the Pithlachascottee River in New Port Richey, the next county up. He said June's daddy, Ezra Carter lived there full time.

I said, "I like Cash's stuff. But, y'know he didn't write *Ring of Fire*. June Carter wrote it before she married Cash."

"No kidding, I thought Cash wrote it," said the Pasco guy. "I knew it was a big hit. I never could understand the sense or meaning of that song. You?"

I said, "I don't know how true it is but I heard June Carter wrote *Ring of Fire* one night after she mistook a tube of Bengay Cream for her hemorrhoid medicine."

After he quit laughing he said, "Cash's place is west of the main drag on Pier Road. You ought to go by in uniform, tell Cash you got songs he needs to hear. He'll be relieved you're not there to confiscate his pharmaceutical stash." Dang, that sounded like an innovative idea. A uniform always bought a little time and attention, right? What if I just walked up to John Cash and told him in so many words I'd written *Gator Bar* for him and the least he could do was hear it. Then once he heard it, he'd have to say he liked it, and that he'd record it and then we'd have a hit on our hands. I'd have residuals coming in hand over fist and I could quit my job and do as I damned well pleased. It worked for Roger Miller. If he could get a hit with *You Can't Go Roller Skating In A Buffalo Herd,* well . . .

The traffic was light on US-19 as I tooled along past closed gas stations and darkened citrus groves. Low on the eastern horizon, somewhere over Old Tampa Bay, heat lightning promised more rain. The weather was puckering up to do something, somewhere. Wedged in the seat was my portable radio pumping out Sunny James's *Only the Lonely* and Cash's newest hit *Boy Named Sue.* Tapping the steering wheel, keeping time with Luther Perkin's guitar licks, my mind drifted back again to song-writing.

Flipping on my high beams, I was jolted from my reverie by a pale apparition moving slowly in knee-high weeds alongside the hardtop. Walking tediously with arms crossed, the figure presented an eerie sight in the glow of oncoming traffic. Slightly built, she was dressed entirely in white.

Why would a female be walking the highway at this late hour, vulnerable, miles from anywhere? I slowed and stopped. She quickly opened the passenger door and stooped to look inside. I turned on the interior light and asked, "Lady, what the hell you doing out here walking around in the middle of night?"

Placing a shaky hand on the car door and the other on the roof, the woman leaned in. Her eyes were clear but expressed panic. She said, simply, "My husband's trying to kill me."

I'd been a deputy for a long time and cynically believed I'd seen or heard every sort of grievance and violent tale there was to tell. Hearing again such tribulations from this stranger, seemingly augmented by alcohol, I pointed at the S.O. radio and said, "I'm a Pinellas Deputy, ma'am. Get in and I'll take you down to Gulf-to-Bay (Boulevard) and we'll sort this out. I can get Clearwater P.D. to hook up with us, maybe take you home. Let's see what we can do."

I called radio, advised I had a white female "10–12" that she was alone, walking south on US-19. I should have taken this woman's story seriously. What is that old maxim; no good deed goes unpunished?

Drunk or sober, Jack Travis (not his real name) was one mean sonofabitch. Even folks that didn't know him gave him a wide berth, same as they would a myopic cottonmouth. No one had anything good to say about him. He made a living working in cement and neighbor Hugh Kearny, alluding to his brute strength, said he watched from his kitchen window one morning as Jack Travis single handedly wrestled a three or four hundred pound concrete encrusted mixing trough into the bed of his truck.

Very little was known of his upbringing or his family background, only that he had come to Pinellas County from Alabama. He drank hard and lived violent. He enjoyed other people's misery. Even unprovoked he would beat on his wife or step kids.

Earlier in the day, during the five o'clock cocktail hour, he had unexpectedly walked into the Pelican Restaurant, an old, established Clearwater Beach eatery. He was there to fetch his waitress wife Ruby who was to come with him "Right now! An' by gawd, I mean now!" He gave no reason. That was sufficient. He justified his actions to no one. Walking out the front door, Ruby meekly waved to owner Henry Henriquez and, like a faithful old hound, followed Jack into the parking lot. They climbed into his Pontiac Bonneville and left the beach.

Other than what she said later, it was unknown how the two spent the better part of the evening. But, they ended up at the Turf Bar in Oldsmar, a seasonal haunt for horse owners, jockeys, and race track laborers. Jack had little truck with those hardworking transients but was acquainted with owner Ted Salute and preferred boozing there where his outrageous behavior was tolerated more than anywhere else.

Jack was an open Mason jar of nitro. A young man, who had once worked with Ruby at a Winn Dixie Grocery Store, greeted her as she sat with Jack at the Turf Bar. Twice the boy's age and three times his size, Jack flew into a blind rage and beat the kid unmercifully. He ruptured the youth's spleen, fractured his jaw, and dislodged his front teeth with his steel toed work shoes. Unconscious and bleeding, the boy was whisked off the premises by friends. No one called the law, no one wanted to cross big bad Jack Travis.

Why do some men cling to their hate and anger? How do they sustain the acrimony, the rage that becomes their manna, their mantra? Their souls fester, and stagnate as rotted matter in a cesspit. Distorted, perverted. How do they come into this world, these men who look no different than you or me? Were they born incensed or tormented as an abhorrent chained spirit? Some are clever and tenacious. Some possess the dimness of a night serpent. They are out there, men who romp with the devil. You pass them every day . . . within arm's reach, on the street and in public places. Often they are men with clean hands and corrupt values, and strangers never know.

Ted Salute would testify at the coroner's jury he overheard Jack tell Ruby, as a matter-of-fact, that he intended to kill her before midnight. He didn't hear the reason. But, Ruby, a little tipsy by now, showed no sign of defying her husband so the bar owner wasn't overly concerned. He'd heard it all before. Jack Travis spent his drinking hours expressing extreme displeasure with cops, his bosses, and society in general. He often said his motto in life was, "The more you bitch, the longer God lets you live." So, tonight his usual drunken ramblings were judged as just that; drunken rambling threats. Ted couldn't tell whether the big man was carrying a gun but like a wounded gator Jack Travis was dangerous when drunk and brooding. He said one drink was too many for Jack and a hundred, not enough. There was a fight in every shot of bourbon.

Richard Nixon was president, Johnny Cash had a hit show on ABC TV, *Get Back* was the Beatles latest hit, and the quintessential hippy flick *Easy Rider* starring Peter Fonda, Dennis Hopper, and Jack Nicholson had just been released. In the next few days nearly a half-million long haired, dope smoking, acid dropping, advocates of free love would invade Bethel, New York to hear Richie Havens, Joan Baez, and Arlo Guthrie sing protest songs condemning the still raging war in Viet Nam. The event would be forever known as Woodstock.

Remarkably on this night a military transport had lifted off Tan Son Nhut Air Base near Saigon, headed for America. Among the two hundred weary troops aboard was a young combat-hardened marine coming home to Clearwater with a single objective gnawing at his gut. He was going to kill Jack Travis. He knew how. The skills for which he had been trained and had utilized during two tours in the jungles of Viet Nam would provide the expertise to get the job done.

But, what was about to unfold in the next few minutes would render the Marine's mission unnecessary—actually impossible.

I suppose, this is where *coincidence* comes into play. Inexplicably, the young warrior and I would meet up after I'd left the sheriff's office. The American Heritage dictionary defines coincidence as the "accidental occurrence of events that seem to have a connection." I'll let you make that judgment call.

CHAPTER TWO

"Does Your Husband Have a Gun?"

THE WOMAN DROPPED INTO the front seat like a bag of loose marbles and slammed the door. She had been pummeled and battered. Heading south, she told me her name was Ruby Jean Travis. Her husband Jack had forced her to leave her waitress job on Clearwater Beach and they had gone to Oldsmar on the other side of the county to Ted Salute's Turf Bar. Jack had been drinking since early afternoon, after leaving his construction job. She said the more he drank, the more she was convinced he intended to harm her. She could give no reason for his violence, could provide no logic, no rationale. He was just a "nasty bastard." While telling me her story her composure disintegrated. Clearly the woman was terrified. She began to babble.

A car's headlights locked in close on my car, less than three feet from my back bumper. Keeping an eye on the rear-view mirror, I asked, "Does your husband have a weapon . . . a gun . . . on him or in the car?" Ruby wasn't all that sure. She didn't think he was carrying a gun on his person, "But, he keeps one in the car, under the seat."

As she rambled on, I began rethinking this guy, convinced he was indeed an unreasonable nasty bastard. My dad would have called him a bad actor.

I watched in the rear-view mirror as the distinctive grill of a Pontiac stayed dangerously close to the back of my unmarked car which bore the standard bright yellow reflective sheriff's license plate. When headlights hit that official license plate, particularly up close and just right, it glared like the sun. I asked the make of her husband's car. Ruby said it was a fairly new Pontiac. Okay, I had an angry husband and possibly a gun totin' drunk to contend with. I got on the horn to dispatch. "Car 89."

Ernie Hutchinson, the radio operator, answered, "Car 89. Go ahead."

"Ten-four, Ernie, I got a domestic up here . . . ah . . . the wife's 10–12 (with me). She's been knocked around a bit. She's all right. Said the subject . . . her husband . . . has threatened to kill her. I'm south bound on U.S. 19, coming up on (State Road) 590. The subject is riding my bumper, not backing off. How about getting a uniform car to 10–56 (meet) me up here somewhere? The wife is not certain . . . subject could be armed. Maybe, you should get a second uniform car and a supervisor up here, as well. 10–4?"

Uniform deputy Mike Petruccelli broke in on the radio, "Car 89, I'm just south of Belleair Road, headed your way. What's your 10–20 (location)?"

I was stopped at the traffic light at Old Coachman Road. "Mike, the wife is 10–12; the husband's driving a late model Pontiac, light blue. He's gonna be a problem."

I felt a touch of relief. Mike Petruccelli was a kick-ass guy and headed my way like the Second Cavalry. I knew Mike enjoyed a good scrap. He liked mixing it up. I needed backup and Mike was the man, he was fearless.

"Radio?"

"Go ahead, 89."

"How about checking . . . see if we have warrants . . . anything outstanding on a white male Jack H. Travis. Standby a minute Ernie."

I turned to Ruby, "What's your husband's D.O.B., date of birth?"

She shrugged her thin shoulders, "I don't know. He's thirty eight. I'm seven years older than him."

"Ernie, don't have a D.O.B. He's around thirty-eight years of age."

Radio responded, "Ten-four, I'll check the card file, standby."

The traffic light changed and I slowly accelerated. From the corner of my eye I saw the Pontiac leap forward. It whipped across three lanes and with a bone jarring crunch, sideswiped my car. This was before seat belts and air bags. Jolted, I hit the brakes and slid to a stop, teetering on the muddy edge of a deep drainage channel running parallel to the highway. The blue Pontiac shot past me, careened recklessly down into the ditch and came to a roaring halt in knee deep water. Angry clouds of churning steam rolled up and around the bigger car. Regaining my wits, I glimpsed through the swirling vapors a large, bulky male climb from the Pontiac and clamber up the slick, mucky embankment heading in my direction.

The woman, pounding her fists on the door lock, screamed, "He'll kill you . . . he don't care who you are! He'll kill you and me!" Scrunching down in the front seat, she made herself small, as if to hide, she whimpered, "Jack's gonna have his gun."

Earlier, I had believed she was overreacting. Now, I knew better.

By the same token, I knew this was one ol' boy he sure as hell wasn't gonna kill. I reached inside my coat and unsheathed my shiny, well-oiled Smith & Wesson. I was confident the black snubbed-nose was loaded, but out of habit, I rolled the cylinder for assurance and opened the car door.

Experts will tell you a gun is the only personal weapon that puts a 95-pound woman on equal footing with a 220–pound rapist or a 75-year old retiree on equal footing with a 22-year old crack-head, or one deputy on equal footing with a carload of drunks with base-ball bats. The gun removes the disparity in physical strength, size, or numbers between a potential attacker and a defender.

Being left handed, I held my weapon in that hand and my ID in the other, and loudly informed the approaching big man, who appeared empty handed, that I was a deputy sheriff and that he was under arrest. He closed in. He had the eyes of a predator. Reading body language and facial expressions is a form of intuition. It's called profiling. We all do it, both cops and civilians. Babies do it instinctively. In my uneducated opinion, it's probably in grade school and high school that we sharpen that instinct. We do it consciously or unconsciously every hour of the day. It's human nature. Some cops acquire it quicker than others. Some never do. If a cop fails to develop these skills experientially, he will fail to be effective. Instinct told me to buckle-up—this was one bad sonofabitch. I could have ended it then and there. I should have ended it right then. But, he was not armed. Because I was armed, an asinine thought crossed my mind, *this is not gonna be a fair fight.* How smart is that? I should have fired one off. He was gonna piss in my oatmeal.

After years of "carrying the tin" (badge) I was instilled with a heavy dose of self-confidence; it's called the Duke Wayne syndrome. When you mix in a large measure of ego, the possibility of getting one's skinny butt stomped becomes a possibility. Complicate this equation with an emotional attempt to deal justly with a volatile and crazy human being; I violated the first and primary tenet of a fight; to never ever let something or someone that threatens you to get inside arm's length. It was a critical and stupid blunder on my part. It would cost me, big time.

Watching the guy approach, I sensed he was even worse news. But, I didn't have to speculate, Ruby Jean had told me enough already. Physically I was in good shape, but was certain I couldn't take this guy, one-on-one.

Without so much as an "up-yours," he put a hit to my face that knocked me backwards, off balance. Had I not slammed up against my car I would have gone down. My ID flew out of my hand but, like Linus and his security blanket, I had a death grip on my weapon. Professionally I'd been in scrapes and tussles with big guys and little guys and mean guys, you name it. But most often I was not alone. I usually had backup or was helping out a fellow officer. I did get punched once by an inebriated biker babe at the Old Boardwalk Tavern on Haines Road. She knocked my pearly white "good guy" Stetson square off my bean and into the gravel. But the hit I took this time was rock hard. It hurt.

Previous experiences had taught me there were two ways of dealing with a violent human being: reason or force. Reasoning with this freak had just gone down the toilet. From the get-go he had crossed the line, committing a felony, by deliberately sideswiping my car. Now blindly, he was taking me on, an armed lawman. His instincts were that of a rabid animal.

What must I have been thinking, exactly? Did I really want to shoot this maniac? I was justified, lawfully, but I searched my harried mind for an alternative?

Travis had me by 25 or 30 pounds. He was older, stockier . . . boozed up and his adrenaline and testosterone were boiling, pumping. He worked in concrete, heavy construction. He was dressed in jeans and a T-shirt. I was 175 pounds, wearing a suit and tie. I was sober, physically fit, but he was one hell of an adversary. Without a weapon my odds would not have been good. Without weapons, confrontations are won by the physically superior individual inflicting overwhelming injury on the loser. But I had a six shooter. He didn't.

He hit me again. I wobbled but stayed upright. Quickly recovering, I stood protectively with my butt and shoulders hugging my car. He came on me with the force of a five-ton forklift and tore blindly at my throat and eyes, ramming me against my vehicle. A rush of adrenaline shoved me into afterburner. I took a deep breath and with my one free hand forced him off me. How I found the strength to do that I'll never know. He came back on me. I was battling this maniac with one hand and losing, big time. With the wind knocked out of me, he was cutting off my air . . . had me by the throat.

One might ask why anyone, particularly a lawman, would allow this viciousness to continue when they have the tool, the skill and the ability to stop it. Good question. I feared the act of taking a life regardless of the abuse I was experiencing.

I broke away, yet he slugged me repeatedly with hits to the face and upper body. I staggered like a drunk. For a split second tiny lights, like a child's whirling sparkler, twinkled in my head. I pushed to keep Travis from getting in close but he was relentless. We shuffled around, moving constantly. Then the scrap slipped into slow motion and I became infinitely aware I was on my own in this struggle. It was just me and him, John Ford's cavalry wasn't going to ride in at the last moment like in the flick *Rio Grande*. I became definitively logical and acutely aware. I began to reason, yet I still wondered . . . "Where . . . is . . . Petruccelli? He . . . should . . . have . . . been . . . here . . . by . . . now."

I knew Ruby Travis, the woman in white, was standing at the other side of my car, watching. I thought it strange, why wasn't she doing something— anything? As the free-for-all continued no words were uttered. There were no expressions of acrimony. It was radical combat, yet curiously silent. He was intent on killing me. I was laboring to prevent it. How weird and abnormal it all seemed. After I'd identified myself no words were exchanged. It was akin to two struggling Alfa animals in the dark . . . beating the hell out of one another. My death was his intent.

Again, he had me by the throat. My lights were fading. I was getting light headed. I would have gone to my knees had we not been belly-to-belly, gut-to-gut, me between him and the car. He reeked of stale liquor, tobacco, and sweat. I struggled for air, just to catch short breathes. Yet, fighting to stay alive, I don't recall having fear. Fear was never a factor. My anger mounted, and then it turned to rage. It was time for this BS to cease. This goofy bastard had been given every chance, every opportunity.

Years later I watched the TV series *Lonesome Dove*. In one scene Robert Duval was alone, pinned down by the far-off guns of a renegade Comanche mob. Hunkered down behind his dead horse, a wild slug pinged dangerously close to his head, nicking his saddle horn.

Like Duvall, I finally told myself, "Now–by–God–this—has–gone–far–enough!" The time had come to hammer this devil to hell, to *gut up* and ratchet down.

It's been said the average lawman is a mediocre shot or worse. But the guys I worked with were competent gun handlers, good shots and "handy with a shootin' iron." I held my own at the range with and against other guys in the department. Occasionally I liked spending extra time at the range with civilian buddies to shoot other types of weapons. I easily qualified each year.

The standard pull on a Smith & Wesson revolver is between 12 and 14 pounds.

In this case, I couldn't miss.

I shoved the short steel barrel hard against that soft spot just below Jack's right rib cage and lit one off. There was a violent, lightning quick impact. The weapon going off between two bodies, two struggling masses of muscle, blood and bone carried a deadly consequence.

He stepped back. I thought it was over. I slid to the trunk area of my car and worked at regaining my balance and bearing, to stay upright and catch a full breath. He came back on me. The quick hot blast seemed only to infuriate the big man who grunted and swore at me. He returned to the foray with renewed rage. I was again slammed up and over the trunk of my car, my toes barely touching the ground. He was clawing at my neck, and working hard to earn the Golden BB.

Until then, as a deputy, I had foolishly believed I was indestructible. Nothing could harm or kill me. I was the good guy. Youthful ignorance dictated that when I wore a white uniform shirt and Stetson, that a badge stopped bullets. Big bullets, little bullets, it didn't matter. I was the man of steel. Now I was in civvies. Reality kicked in. I'm thinking, *"What am I doing here anyway? How the hell did I allow this crap to get this far?"*

He tried head-butting me, and then just as his head moved to the level of my throat I fired a second round, slanting the shot down, into his torso. He backed off, called me a sonofabitch and came back on me for the third time. We tumbled and slid 15 – 20 feet to the bottom of the ditch. On top of me, he began pushing my head under the brackish water.

He had two slugs in him. Should I fire another round? Would it do any good? What were the chances? Would the snake never die?

For whatever reason, I knew Ruby was still standing directly at the top of the hill beside the car. I thought it futile to fire a third round. What if it went wild? Had I mistakenly loaded up with snake-shot? In the blackness, I lashed out and hammered my weapon where I knew his head to be. I struck behind his right ear. The repeated, powerful whacks took effect. He slowed, moaned, and went limp. I pulled myself out from under the dead weight. The body dropped back; face down in the brackish stream. I was breathing fast and heavy. One wonders what a person is thinking in the last seconds of life, what is going through this man's mind. I heard a slow gurgling sound. The dark form at my feet was taking in the filthy water.

Bloomp. Bloomp. Bloomp.

It was a desperate soft sound. I thought to myself the only way he's gonna come out of that water is by his own muscle. The contest was over. I had won my stripes. I had fought the good fight and survived. He hadn't.

There are moments of finality that we encounter, moments when the hammer is down, the curtain closed, the drapes drawn, the lights darkened. It is a black and shadowy world like a Poe novel, thick with tangible gloominess similar to an old Kodak negative. Wet grass will never smell the same.

I was one fortunate son of a gun. I kept telling myself I should never have allowed the guy to get that close. Hindsight is always 20–20. I'd been stupidly reckless but exceptionally lucky. Luck is a force that brings good fortune. It favors chance. There's the old adage: I'll take luck over skill any day.

I could not feel pity for this man, this other human being. If anything, there was raw anger. I was outraged that he had put me in such a foul position. I have replayed the incident a thousand times in my head, and a thousand times I have come to the same conclusion that there was nothing else I could have done. I always accepted that my job was risky. Thank God I was not a rookie. I guess, in Jack's savage world he got what was coming to him. One of the old timers with the department told me later, "The bastard just needed killin.'"

George McNally grew up in New York City's notorious Hell's Kitchen and was one of my FTOs (field training officer). He'd also been my lieutenant in vice. Early on he'd told me if I found myself in a situation using deadly force; never assume one slug would do the trick of taking someone down. He said, "The toothpaste is out of the tube. With that first shot you've committed yourself, you can't take it back. You can't put the bullet back in the gun so give 'em a couple more for good measure. It's good business."

Exhausted, and shaken, and on the verge of hyperventilating, I hauled myself up through the wet weeds to my car, wondering where and how I called up that kind of strength? I was fortunate to be alive. I hurt everywhere and so bad I was cross eyed. I opened the driver's side door and mechanically placed my broken gun in the glove box and closed it. The cylinder had been knocked an eighth of in an inch out of line. I suppose I thought placing the gun in the glove box was essential in preserving evidence, the crime scene. In moments like that, when the mind is numb and cluttered, who the hell knows?

Adrenaline is a potent brew until it runs out. Thank God I'd started out with a substantial quota. Still out of breath and working hard to keep my voice stone cold and emotionless I got on the radio and said calmly that I needed a supervisor and an ambulance, 10–18 (*immediately!*), at a location just south of Coachman Road on the west side of US-19.

I surprised myself. My voice sounded strong and even. I was still in control although my mouth was dry as paper and thousands of wasps were buzzing in my head.

Ernie Hutchinson, an experienced radio operator and former St. Petersburg motorcycle cop, asked, "Whatta ya got up there 89?"

I was mindful that some deputies in times of high stress yelled and spoke hastily over the radio. I tried keeping my mind clear and spoke clearly while repeating my request for a supervisor and an ambulance, 10–18. I was reluctant to relay details because our radio transmissions were monitored and recorded by the media and other police agencies throughout the Tampa Bay area.

Mike Petruccelli came in over the air, "Daryl. I'm about 10–97." He was seconds away. In reply, I clicked the mike twice, a deputy's way of acknowledging another's transmission.

I looked through the car's open doors at Ruby Travis. She stared back and asked, "Is he dead?" I didn't answer. I was distracted, listening to the far-off scream of Petruccelli's Ford cruiser as he cleared the railroad overpass north of Drew Street.

At that moment, I sensed someone at my back, very close. A Florida Highway Trooper was standing there. I didn't know him. He had to have seen the S.O. license plate. He asked, "What's the problem?"

I was beaten, hurting, impatient, exhausted, soaking wet, muddy, bloody, and pissed off. I pointed down into the blackness. "I just shot that wacko bastard . . . down there." Absentmindedly I asked, "Is (troopers) Jim Hooks or Barnwell working tonight?" He didn't answer.

It's difficult to feel remorseful for someone who had just tried their all-out, level best to end your life. And thinking about it—the guy wasn't all that bright either. Drunk or sober anyone with half a brain wouldn't assault a lawman, especially a lawman holding a gun. I never thought of myself as really a bad ass, but I was exceedingly pissed and had been functioning on an overdose of anger and adrenaline.

Gripping a six-cell flashlight on his shoulder the trooper turned and directed a bright circle of light down onto Travis's form lying half-submerged in the water. The trooper emitted a thin whistle through his front teeth—a whistle that started with a "P" and followed with a whispered, "Holy shh-hit!"

By chance, a nurse and her male companion saw the Pontiac sideswipe me, had followed, and then stopped to see what was going on. They stood listening to my conversation with the trooper. Unknown to me, the man was an auxiliary deputy and recognized me. The trooper and nurse sloshed down into the mud and pulled Jack's body out of the water and attempted to restore life. He was past the point of saving.

Jack Travis died cheap.

Mike Petruccelli roared up and promptly secured the scene. Minutes later, Sheriff Genung arrived and ordered that the area be covered with detectives and uniform deputies. By chance and good fortune, nine people had actually witnessed the incident.

Uniform deputy M. A. "Mike" Petruccelli filed the following report: Writer received a call at 23:21 hrs. on August 7, 1969 that Deputy Daryl May was requesting assistance at the intersection of SR-590 and US-19. Writer arrived at the location around 23:37 hrs. and met with Deputy May who asked writer to check on the ambulance and have a supervisor come to the scene. Writer called and then went back to the scene, and viewed the body for the first time. The body was on its back and slanted backwards into the ditch. Writer kept all persons away until Lt. Jerry Coleman took charge of the scene. Writer handled traffic thereafter.

Two or three righteous cynics rode in on white horses. Others formed unsubstantiated opinion without being there, hoping I'd been caught screwing around with the wife of a jealous husband. They were disappointed. Not too long ago, one ex-deputy, in a fit of resentfulness, aired his feelings to me about Jack Travis's death. Telling about that issue is still to come.

Miss Ruby wasn't my cup of tea.

AS WORD FILTERED OUT over the air, my good friends arrived to lend moral support. Lt. Gerry Coleman, later to become sheriff, Detective Frank Holloway, now a retired major, hustled me to the back seat of an unmarked car. Also present was Leigh McEachern, a former St. Pete vice detective, who would become chief deputy with the Orange County Sheriff's Office (Orlando). We'd watched each other's back on several occasions. My longtime trusted partner Bruce Little also showed up. We'd worked together in uniform and consorted in Vice & Intelligence. Now a civilian, he had left the department to attend college and later became a Special Agent with the FBI.

Sheriff Genung arrived and instructed me to go to the Sheriff's Administration Building, downtown Clearwater. Before leaving I asked Holloway to retrieve my D-28 Martin guitar from the trunk of my damaged Ford.

Later, Holloway told me that Uniform Captain Carl McMullen, a cigar clenched in his teeth, kneeled, pulled back the shroud covering Travis's lifeless form and muttered, "Well, there's one bad ass (that) won't be (expletive) with a skinny deputy anymore!"

At the administration building the sheriff was bent on me giving a sworn statement. He said statements had been secured from other witnesses, that, "There were two women that saw the whole thing from the liquor store parking lot across the highway." Even Jack Travis's wife provided detailed information in a favorable sworn statement. He was adamant on wrapping up the case that night.

I had a lot of confidence in myself and a strong faith in the legal system. I was experienced at thinking on my feet and countering unanticipated questions thrown at me by court room prosecutors, defense lawyers, and judges. Even confrontations with inane judges like Richard Kelly, who suffered a severe case of "robitis", and ultimately ended up in the federal slammer due to his participation in the Abscam fiasco, didn't rattle me.

But I had always dealt with the actions of others, what they'd done, why they had done it, what I had observed and found in my investigations. Now the focus was not on some defendant but on me. It was an entirely different scenario. It was me and the action I'd taken, what I'd done. There would be a close and critical examination of my actions and the reasons I'd taken a life.

I was apprehensive but confident I'd made correct decisions, that my actions were justified. Wasn't a lawyer the first thing a perp started yelling for when they thought they were in trouble? Getting a lawyer—a good lawyer—made a lot of sense. It made sense to my friends. I needed to know where I stood legally. What should I do? How should I do it? I needed the guidance of a professional, an expert defense lawyer.

Loyd Mosely was the best.

Coleman phoned Mosely, got him out of bed, and explained the circumstances. Loyd said he'd be at the SAB (Sheriff's Administration Building) in 20 minutes.

Sheriff Genung was losing patience. "Damn it," he persisted, "We've got this shoot tied-up, son. We can take this to a coroner's jury first thing tomorrow."

At any other time I would have trusted Genung with my life. He was a savvy lawman and a sheriff that didn't make idiotic political decisions.

"Boss," Coleman said, "I called Loyd Mosely . . . he's on his way. That's all we need, just half an hour."

Shortly, Loyd strolled in and came directly to me, asked a few questions, and then said to the sheriff, "Don, your guy's been through hell tonight, you know that. I'm not gonna let him give a statement. We'll have plenty of time in the morning. What's the hurry? We'll talk it over in the morning and get an idea where we stand with all this."

Loyd and the sheriff were respected friends. He smiled at the sheriff and said, "Don, you know this is the right thing to do. Let's adjourn. Whataya say?"

On the night of the shooting Sheriff's Detective Frank Coleman filed the following report: Writer arrived at the scene (involving Det. Daryl May) shortly before midnight and assisted in preserving the scene until Sheriff Genung and other supervisors arrived.

While at the Sheriff Admin. Building, writer (Det. Coleman) was told by the victim's wife that her husband was drunk this night, and stated that it usually takes three (3) good men to subdue her husband when he gets in this condition.

On 07/17/1966 writer (Det. Coleman) arrested the victim, Jack Travis for attempting to elude a police officer. This occurred during the late evening hours when writer observed a white T-Bird speeding north on Belcher Road. Writer observed a second auto driving recklessly in pursuit of the T-Bird, and after using red light and siren, writer finally stopped the second vehicle (white Pontiac) at the corner of Belcher Road and Palmetto Street. The driver of the vehicle was Jack Travis. He had been drinking at the time. It was also learned that he had busted up the Wine Cellar minutes before this wild chase. The driver of the T-Bird was Mrs. Ruby Lee Travis who later came down to the scene of the accident and advised that she was being chased by her husband, and that she was actually attempting to get away from him, fearing her safety at that time.

ST. PETERSBURG TIMES
Fatal Shooting Inquest Set

August 9, 1969

CLEARWATER—Approximately a dozen witnesses have been subpoenaed to testify here Monday at a 3:30 P.M. inquest into the fatal Thursday night shooting of a Clearwater resident by a Pinellas Sheriff's detective.

A coroner's jury impaneled by District 2 Justice of the Peace David F. Patterson, will sift facts in the shooting of Jack E. Travis, 35, by deputy detective Daryl May.

ON DUTY in plainclothes and driving an unmarked Sheriff's Department vehicle at the time of the incident, May, 33, said he shot Travis, after Travis grappled with him in an attempt to choke him. The incident occurred near U.S. 19 just south of State Road 590 (Coachman Road).

In a recap of the shooting, Pinellas Sheriff Don Genung described Jack E. Travis as a 200–pounder with a record of local arrests for assault and battery, rape, attempting to elude police, reckless driving and marital troubles, which brought other deputies to his home six times so far this year. Travis was dead on arrival at Morton F. Plant Hospital shortly after midnight. Travis has an extensive FBI record, Genung said.

A Florida Highway Patrolman investigated the accident phases of the incident, and administered mouth-to-mouth resuscitation to Travis before he was taken to the hospital.

GENUNG said Travis and his wife were involved in an argument earlier Thursday evening at the Pelican Restaurant on Clearwater Beach where Mrs. Ruby Lee Travis is employed as a waitress. Two other altercations between Travis and his wife occurred later at two separate bars, Genung said.

Witnesses scheduled to testify at the Monday inquest include Dr. James O. Norton, North Pinellas County medical examiner, Mrs. Travis, Harold B. Foster and Frances E. Nurrenrbroch, both of

New Port Richey. Roxanne Grimsley, a waitress at the Turf Bar in Oldsmar; Ted Salute, owner of the Turf, and three sheriff's deputies.

THE MORNING AFTER THE SHOOT, I awoke to read the report in the *St. Petersburg Times and Tampa Tribune.* After breakfast with my family I assured my kids that their dad was okay. I went to the Clearwater office and was pulled aside by Captain Ella Leon, head of the civil division. She asked how I was doing, if my family was all right, and had I gotten enough rest.

I felt okay, although I had a busted lip and black and blue bruises around my neck, face and upper body. I was a little sore, but okay.

Ella asked if I was wearing that "nice suit" she saw me in yesterday afternoon?

I said, "Yes, mam, the suit was ruined . . . a lot of mud and blood."

She said, "I'm happy it was someone else's blood." She said she had spoken with Florence Genung, the sheriff's wife and his personal secretary, and the sheriff suggested I go to Shorts, a fashionable clothing store for men, and pick out a suit, shirt, shoes, and tie. He asked that I not spend more than a set amount of money on the suit.

First chance I got, I slipped over to Shorts and found a great looking Hart Schaffner Marx on the sales rack. I called Mrs. Genung and told her I'd found the perfect dark suit, and that I'd pay the extra $25. I stayed on the phone while she spoke with the sheriff. She came back on, said, "Daryl, Don said for you to get that suit; he'll cover the extra cost." I left with a handsome suit, a new tie and shirt. I was going to look presentable for the coroner's inquest.

Chief Deputy Bill Roberts wanted to know if I wanted my gun repaired or replaced. I told him, for sentimental reasons, I'd prefer the gun be repaired. But, if the gun couldn't be fixed and if the department bought me a new gun, I wanted a .44 Magnum with a four foot barrel.

INQUEST: The inquest was set for the following Tuesday. On that day, Mrs. Genung called me at home, "Daryl, Don wants you to come by the office a few minutes before the inquest. He wants to walk over to the court house with you, all right?"

At midmorning I walked into the sheriff's expansive office. I ached all over. It was painful to swallow, painful to smile. My head ached and my face, neck and chest were splotched. I had no serious cuts or broken bones, although my nose had been pushed and bent a couple times. Even my weapon was busted up, broken.

The sheriff yelled, "Come in here, son!" He stood up, leaned over his desk, looked me over and asked, "Is that my new suit?" I said it was. "Is that my new shirt?" I said it was. "Is that my new tie?" Yes. "Where are my new shoes?" I told him I was unable to find suitable shoes in time for the inquest. "They were just too expensive at Shorts, boss."

"You alright?" I said I was.

Genung differed, "No you're not. You came from a good family; you have a strong Christian background; and this shoot is troubling for you. But God's commandment is not 'thou shalt not kill.' It's 'thou shalt not murder.' Son, you prevented your own murder." That made a lot of sense, something I needed to hear, to think about. That night . . . and the nights to follow . . . I slept like a baby.

As we headed out the door Mrs. Genung smiled and wished me luck. Waiting on the steps of what is now the old courthouse was Allan Allweise, one of the several prosecutors with the State Attorney's office. He was and probably remains an aggressive little guy. His know-how and attitude made up for his size. It was going to be his job to conduct the inquest. His investigator, Denny Quilligan stood close by. We walked inside the court house and Allweise, feisty and combative, filled us in on procedure, what to expect, how the witnesses and testimony would be presented. I was glad he was on my side.

Abruptly he glanced over my shoulder towards the north street entrance. Ruby Travis was walking in with an attorney. Allweise brushed past me and pointed his finger in the face of the lawyer. His voice echoed in the vacant halls, "I know why you're here, Bryce. Let me tell you right now . . . if that bitch gets up there and lies I'll charge her with perjury. She's given a sworn statement about this shoot and its iron clad."

Allweise implied the Travis family had a civil suit in mind and was going for compensation.

Judge David Patterson was on the bench. I'd known him for years. We often greeted each other by first name. This day he was all business and rarely looked at me. I understood, but it was uncomfortable, awkward.

Oddly, at that moment, I recalled something else Lt. George McNally told me when I was a rookie. He said, if and when a critical moment ever came and your weapon has to be used just remember one simple tenet, "It is better to be up there in front of the judge explaining why you put a guy away than having the bad guy telling a jury of twelve why he put your lights out."

An elderly black lady who witnessed the shoot from the liquor store parking lot across the highway was the first witness to be sworn in. She said the big car sideswiped the little car. She said, "They was a whole lot of scufflin' goin' on between two men . . . they were banging and thrashin' around over there."

Other witnesses took the stand and gave sworn testimony that coincided with the facts as I remembered them. Finally I was called to the stand. Allen Allweise began by advising me of my rights. I looked at the sheriff. The sheriff looked straight back at me. I knew that he knew what I was feeling; that events had reached a pretty serious stage.

ST. PETERSBURG EVENING INDEPENDENT
Deputy Cleared in Fatal Shooting

Tuesday, August 12, 1969

"It's a terrific shock," said Pinellas County Sheriff Don Genung this morning while describing how Deputy Daryl May felt after killing a man.

"No one has thought about how May felt about this," said the sheriff.

It's a terrific shock for a man in this business . . . when he has done all he can to save his own life and then can do nothing else but shoot a man to death."

"You don't get over it easily. He and his whole family are very upset," said the sheriff.

ST. PETERSBURG TIMES CITY EDITION
Sheriff's Deputy Cleared in Fatal Shooting of Man

Tuesday, August 12, 1969

CLEARWATER—A six man coroner's jury late yesterday returned a verdict of justifiable homicide in the shooting of a Clearwater man by a Pinellas sheriff's detective last Thursday.

The jury said deputy detective Daryl May, 33, was acting in the line of duty and in defense of his own person when he shot and killed Jack E. Travis after a struggle in a ditch on U.S. 19 near State Road 590.

The jury deliberated approximately 35 minutes after hearing testimony from nine witnesses.

THREE WITNESSES—One the owner of an Oldsmar bar which Travis frequented–described the 200–plus pound Travis as a man always looking for trouble, who carried a gun.

Ted Salute, the bar owner, said Travis picked a fight with a customer in his place several weeks ago, "and worked him over pretty good."

"(Travis) was pretty mean," Salute said.

Mrs. Travis testified in hearing only one shot fired and was unsure as to whether the "scuffling," as she put it, took place near the left front door of the detective's (unmarked) cruiser or transpired some 25 feet away in a ditch off the shoulder of the highway.

AT ONE point in her testimony, Mrs. Travis said she "saw and heard one shot." After some examination by Assistant State Attorney Allen Allweiss, Mrs. Travis conceded that the shot she heard and the one she saw was the only shot—and not two shots as testified to earlier by Dr. James Norton, the Pinellas County Coroner.

Mrs. Travis said she saw and heard the shot as she watched May "getting up off John." The testimony conflicted with statements made earlier by May that Travis was holding him down in the watery ditch. But, Mrs. Travis testified later that she wasn't sure where the bulk of the scuffle took place.

Mrs. Travis' testimony also appeared to conflict with that of Salute that Travis was a troublemaker. Mrs. Travis said her husband was "not the type to start trouble," but much of her subsequent testimony dealt with his apparent affinity for barroom brawling and beating her with his fists.

Mrs. Travis said her husband beat her up in a series of recent episodes, one which caused neighbors to call police. Mrs. Travis said her husband forced her to leave her post as a waitress about 6:30 P.M. on the night of the shooting. She said they went to a couple bars—one of them Salute's place—then started to drive home. They each had several beers and, "he (her husband) was pretty loaded."

Mrs. Travis said her husband suddenly parked their late-model Pontiac on the shoulder of U.S. 19 and said, "I'm going to sit here and torture you until five o'clock in the morning."

THE WITNESS said she got out of the car and walked a few feet down the shoulder, when May drove up to inquire what she was doing, "walking on the highway at this time of night."

It was about 11 P.M., she said. May drove a short distance down the highway, after advising Mrs. Travis he was a plain clothes officer.

Another witness, Earl B. Foster of New Port Richey corroborated May's story that Travis's car "tailgated" his cruiser down U.S. 19 to a point just south of Coachman Road (State Road 580) when it swung wide into the inside lane then turned directly into May's unmarked cruiser.

"It was no accident. It was deliberate," Foster testified.

MAY SAID he got out of the cruiser with a pistol in his hand to face Travis, who was walking "hurriedly toward me."

"I told him, 'Hey feller. I'm a deputy sheriff,'" May testified.

May said Travis punched him in the face then grabbed him by the throat with both hands.

"He had me bent back across the rear fender of my vehicle and was choking me. I kept holding the gun out away from me and he kept hitting, so then I put the gun up against him and fired one round. "

"I heard him grunt, but he kept coming at me," May said.

LATER, MAY said, Travis had him down in a ditch partly filled with water. The detective said he fired a second time and heard another grunt "but he stayed right on top of me trying to force my head down (in the water)."

May said he then clubbed Travis a couple times on the back of the head with the butt of his 38 caliber revolver.

"Then he relaxed and I pushed him off me," May said.

Travis was pronounced dead at the scene by Dr. James O. Norton, who later performed an autopsy. Norton said Travis died from internal hemorrhages caused by one chest wound fired "with the muzzle of the gun right against the chest." A second wound in the hip, was superficial, Norton testified.

NOTE: The St. Petersburg Times writer reported the coroner's jury proceedings pretty accurately but slipped-up on a couple points. In reality I fired both shots before the fight ended in the ditch. Secondly, I struck Travis repeatedly with my gun. I struck him with such force that the gun's cylinder was knocked out of line an eighth of an inch. The two spent cartridges in the cylinder were spun 180–degrees to the bottom.

4 KEYS & 4 COINS

Song by Daryl May (1963)

"Death is so final, you stop where you are

And wait for whatever time brings.

Face down in the middle of a black water pond

In a ditch at the back of the bar."

There were questions, of course. A reporter with the *Evening Independent News* asked the sheriff if there would be any kind of board review taken against me for the shooting. Genung scoffed, said I'd nearly lost my life, that he had just bought me a new suit and "I might very well make him a sergeant." I was even cornered by a do-gooder that asked me, "Did you have to kill that man? Couldn't you have just shot him in the leg or shoulder," he sputtered, "or something?" I told the gentleman, "I think you've been watching too much television. I wasn't trained to ride a white charger, like the Lone Ranger, and perform trick shots. I was fighting for my life. With Jack Travis's record of violence, the man was lucky he lived as long as he did."

There are people—usually low-information folks—that have difficulty grasping the realities of life unless it hits them square in the face. They have strong opinions, offered freely, but they are usually the ones that have never had to put their asses on the line for anything perilous.

In life, I've made plenty of mistakes. Probably the same goes for most of us. Yet, most of us live and learn from our mistakes. Some don't. Sometimes our mistakes are trivial and sometimes they are serious. Jack Travis made a serious mistake and he paid for it.

CHAPTER THREE

"I Ain't Going No Wheres With You, Deputy."

WHAT'S THAT OLD ADAGE; what doesn't kill you makes you stronger? Did Custer say that? The dust had scarcely settled on the Travis shooting when I, still going at it serving civil papers and warrants, drove down to the southern part of Pinellas County. I was holding an arrest warrant for the owner of a car repair shop located on a corner of Seminole Blvd. & 54th Ave. The building is still there. I don't remember what the warrant entailed, but I was to take a guy into custody, put him in jail. Dressed in civilian clothes, I strolled in, found my guy standing behind the counter, put the tin on him and in the nicest way I could—which always seemed to work best—informed him that I had a warrant for his arrest, and that he'd be allowed to make bail as soon as I got him to the county jail in Clearwater. He reached under the counter and hauled out a hefty sawed-off, double barreled shotgun and placed it on the counter, pointed in my general direction. I didn't notice the make or gauge of the weapon because the two big black holes at the end of the barrels blocked my view of everything else. He said, "I ain't going no wheres with you, deputy."

Mustering a healthy dose of discretion I backed out of the place and with as much dignity as I could marshal drove to the nearest pay phone (this was before cell phones) and called the airport office and spoke with J. T., the uniform lieutenant on duty. I told him what had just happened and asked that Captain Carl McMullen be informed of my situation ASAP. I'd standby at the church across the street from the repair-shop until backup arrived or I was otherwise directed by radio. I waited for what seemed like a very long time. Radio traffic remained normal. Nothing happened. I sat on my butt dithering.

Growing exasperated, I finally cranked up and drove straight to our St. Pete-Clearwater Airport office. I blistered up the west stairs to the second floor and went gunning for the lieutenant. The moment he saw me, he smacked his forehead (like he needed a V-8), and said he'd totally forgotten me. I slapped the warrant in his shaky hand, suggesting he insert it someplace personal and left the building to cool off. I heard nothing more. It was as though the incident had never happened.

Shortly afterwards, I requested a transfer and the sheriff stuck me in the Youth Aid Bureau (YAB). I called it the Diaper Brigade. I disliked the thankless baby-sitting job, dealing with naughty delinquents, as well as the yahoo sergeant in charge. He was a self-promoting schmoozer, and a social climber that belonged to every yacht and country club south of Walsingham Road. He spent his time sucking up to the sheriff and county personalities while his elderly Jewish secretary handed out assignments and ran the office. She was a sweetheart. He kept his job because no one else wanted it. A month later, I requested a second transfer and went back to uniform. My time was running nigh.

THE KICKERS: I later experienced two incongruous episodes relating to the Travis shooting. The first incident could have been ugly yet it turned out quite comical, illustrating how bad-asses become candy-asses. The second was an uncanny head-scratcher, something straight out of the *Twilight Zone,* leaving me even today reflecting upon *predestination* or the karmic role in our lives.

SEAWAKE INN: The first event happened at the Best Western-SeaWake Inn on Clearwater Beach. I'd left the S.O. to become moderately established as a lounge entertainer in Jacksonville, Nashville, Myrtle Beach, Charlotte, Brunswick, Columbus, and Savannah.

On this particular night, the SeaWake's enticing little show lounge with low comfy chairs and cocktail tables and perfect acoustics held a little over a hundred people. I was working a home crowd, mostly regulars who knew me. As usual, there were cops in attendance. Barbara Neely-May, one of two cocktail waitresses, then married to my brother Gary, was hustling drinks to the crowd standing out in the lobby. This was not uncommon back in the 70s and 80s when customers willingly stood outside on Friday and Saturday nights waiting to get in for the next show.

Part of my show involved interacting with folks in the audience, strangers were my preference. At a table in the middle of the room sat three guys trying hard to look nasty. Barbara said they'd arrived early, were drinking little, seemed misplaced, and had attitudes. Sprawled out, they were taking up more than their share of floor space. Grubby and unsavory, I suspected they were out of their elements and should have been on some back street dive chugga-luggin' long-neckers, blowin' pot, and shooting pool. I needed to find out what was going on with these dudes.

I motioned in their direction and asked, "How're you fellas doing tonight? Where you all hail from?" I got no replies, no reactions just hard-ass stares. The other folks in the room watched.

I spoke quietly over the microphone as if talking to myself, "Well, I guess these ol' boys could be from Lutz or Stone Mountain. Maybe they don't speak the language . . . or maybe they're just horny."

The audience snickered. My motto was, if at first you don't succeed—turn up the volume.

Grinning, I gave another try. Finally one goober drawled, "We stopped by to see how you're doing, ol' buddy. We was good friends with Jack Travis. You remember him, don'tcha sport?" He smiled a rotten tooth smile intending to intimidate.

Well, there you go. These cowboys were friends of the *late* Jack Travis. The first rule of being an effective bad-ass is that you do not go into the other guy's neighborhood—no matter how many sidekicks you've brought along—without knowing the overall number of blasters in the room.

"No kidding?" Says I, grinning, "We all gotta have friends, don't we?" I paused, took a measured sip, looked around the room, pursed my lips and spoke matter-of-factly, "I got friends, too."

With my drink held at arm's length, I extended a damp finger, "See that big handsome fella sitting over there with the gorgeous blonde? That's Tom Colbert. He's my friend and he's a special agent with the Florida Department of Law Enforcement. You got a popper on you tonight, Tommy?"

An impish grin covered Colbert's tanned face. He drawled, "You know me, Daryl, I sleep with my piece." His grin expanded. Pun intended.

I casually waved in another direction, "See that six top over there? Those boys, with their wives, are some of Largo's finest. How 'bout it Joe, are you guys packing?"

Lieutenant Joe Gallenstein answered, "Daryl, we never come, see you without bringin' six shooters."

I pointed at the bar, "Y'see those guys? They're all deputies. That's George McMullen and Warren McNeely . . . and the guy in the blue shirt is my brother Gary. I know damn well they're packin'. Anybody else carryin' a shootin' iron tonight?"

At least eight men and a couple women raised their hands. I think most were civilians just wanting to get in on the act, holding up their paws to show support. That's what friends do, isn't it? It was a million dollar moment watching expressions of amusement around the room and imagining what was going through the minds of our three guests.

Diminutive Tim Donahue, the longtime intuitive Irish barkeep, when speaking, emitted the rasping sound of a coffee-mill. He started his day with a shot of whatever high-test was handy and an unfiltered cigarette. Drunk or sober, he would fight a buzz saw, and drunk or sober, he was some kind of funny. Concerned about his health, Tim once went to the doctor for a checkup. After closing down one night we sat around the bar discussing life in general. Comedian G. David Howard had stopped by for a free one. I asked Tim what he'd learned from his doctor that morning. As usual, Tim was well into the Jameson Triple Distilled. He said, "I'm okay. The doctor told me, I have the body of a 25-year-old football."

I asked, "You mean you have the body of a 25-year-old football player?"

Tim growled, "Whatever."

Tim and I could read each other like digital clocks. With just a look from me, he knew when a customer needed to hit the bricks. So, I gave him *that look* and he stepped from behind the bar and handed the Alfa male the bar tab. There was a definite snap in Timmy's celery. The three gentlemen got the hint, paid up and walked out stiff legged, like dusted roosters. Colbert and a Florida trooper took a back exit to check I.D.s, covering my back.

For as long as I can remember there has been a standard rule for a gunfight. Always bring a gun. Preferably, bring two or three guns. Bring all of your friends who have guns.

THE GOLDEN BEAR: Joe Nickelo was a good looking, velvet voiced Italian who skillfully played a giant F-hole Gibson concert guitar and kicked base peddles. Besides performing in local beach hotels and clubs, Joe toured nationally with the celebrated Glenn Miller Orchestra. He grew weary of traveling the road, doing one-nighters all over what he called Hell's Half Acre. So, he decided to follow his dream and put his life savings into a little pub south of Largo on Starkey Road, near the railroad tracks. He named the place The Golden Bear.

II

He said, "I was a beat up Marine on a military aircraft comin' home from Viet Nam. I'd made up my mind I was gonna kill Jack Travis."

IIIIIIIIIIIIIIIIIIIIIIIIIIIIIIIIIIIIIIIIIIIIIIIIIIIIIIIIIIIIIIIIIIIIIIIIIIIIII

This is where the previously mentioned *coincidence* occurred. I stopped by early one afternoon and found only Joe and his cook in the place. He was pleased to see me, handed over a cold mug of suds, and proceeded to show me around. The place was tastefully decorated with a spacious hardwood dance floor. Five nights a week, in the soft glow of a small red spotlight, Joe created a warm ambiance with his single act, providing a few pleasant hours for those who enjoyed his special kind of smooth laid-back, big band dance music.

As we talked, I noticed a clean-cut young man come in and park himself at the far end of the bar, close to the door. The cook brought him a beer, and he sat staring at the black and white pictures behind the bar depicting Joe's distinguished musical career.

After a while the boy turned on his stool and calmly asked, "You're Daryl May, aren't you?"

I said I was.

He stood and with his left hand pushed his beer mug along the smooth brass bar top to get nearer. He asked, "You don't know who I am, do you?"

Perplexed, yet un-threatened, I answered, "No, I don't think I do. Help me out."

"Sir, I owe you a profound debt of gratitude," it sounded practiced, rehearsed.

"Really? How's that?"

He said, "I was a pretty tired, beat up Marine on a military aircraft comin' home from my last tour in Viet Nam. I'd made up my mind I was gonna kill Jack Travis when I got back. He was my stepdad. I was little when mom married Jack, and he made our lives miserable, a living hell. He came home plastered one afternoon and threw me into a jalousie door. I was about six years old . . . broke my arm in two places. My face was cut up, too. Jack wouldn't let mom have the car, said to take the (expletive) bus. So mom got me to Morton Plant Emergency in a cab. She never called the cops on Jack . . . outta fear, I guess.

"One time I was home from school, sick. He held a cocked .45 to mom's head and told me to watch real close 'cause he was gonna blow her brains all over the sink and refrigerator."

The young man was matter of fact, dry eyed, sober, and unemotional.

"When I got old enough," he said, "I joined the Marines just to get the hell away from Jack. I could never figure out why mom stayed with him. She'd write and tell me all the mean crap he'd be doing to her."

I nodded.

He said, "I had decided after I got mom's last letter that Jack just needed killin'. On the flight coming home that's all I could think about. I had it worked out in my head. I was gonna do it. But, if I'da killed Jack, I'd be in Raiford now. You got done, sir, what I was planning to do . . . I owe you."

The kid was good looking with a strong jaw and penetrating ice-blue eyes. He looked me straight in the eyes, took my hand and gave it a solid Marine squeeze, turned, and walked out. I never knew his name nor did I ever see him again. It was a remarkable and sobering experience.

During the encounter, Joe sat listening. After the young man left, he said he'd never heard anyone speak about killing in such a calm, cool manner. Obviously, he was experienced.

The question will linger forever in my mind; who or what put that kid in Joe's pub on that quiet afternoon?

Was it an accidental occurrence of events? I think not. I believe a coincidence is God's way of remaining anonymous.

It's a terrible thing to take a life. And over the decades I have asked myself if I hate or hated Jack Travis. No, I think not. Did I dislike him? I didn't know him to like or dislike him. How do I feel about him today? I've forgiven him for the appalling act he forced upon me just as I've been forgiven. Am I sorry it happened? Indeed. I'm also grateful it was me and not some young inexperienced deputy that might not have acted accordingly, that might have perished at the hands of Travis. He might or might not have gotten out of prison by now. But the rookie would still be dead.

ADDENDUM: Years after the Jack Travis shooting, one deputy, who shall remain nameless, continues to grouse. He emailed me, saying in part, "I know where you was coming from in Oldsmar and who that guy (Jack Travis) was married to. Some of us know what was going on that night, and you do too."

I had worked alongside this deputy and thought of him as a friend. Yet, I wasn't totally surprised. I'd heard hints of such rumblings but no one had had the courage to confront me face to face. It took years for this fellow to say something, and it was triggered because he misunderstood a lighthearted remark I'd posted on Facebook. He also took the occasion to point out what a lousy cop I had been, that I was a lame entertainer and . . . let's see . . . he said I was full of myself or words to that effect. Dang.

Once a captain's wife, over-scotched, told me straight out that a handful of people at the sheriff's office begrudged me because they felt I was one of Sheriff Genung's fair haired boys, a favorite. I hoped she was right.

But, the former deputy, in question, chose email to accuse me. I decided not to dignify his snarky remarks with a reply. Coming from a former law enforcement colleague, his allegation of wrong doing was unconscionable. His fabrication implied that the late

Sheriff Don Genung played a leading role in covering up a felony. Additionally, his charge recklessly corrupted the integrity of deputies Gerry Coleman, Herb Weller, Carl McMullen, Mike Sharpe, Frank Coleman, Jim Collins, Jim McAllister, Bruce Little, and Frank Holloway to name some of those men involved in the investigation of Jack Travis's death.

Paradoxically, after I had left the sheriff's office this same deputy shot an unarmed youth burglarizing a Tarpon Springs business. I was off somewhere playing the guitar so I'm ignorant of the details or circumstances. I make no judgement call on the matter. Deputy Mike Sharpe told me he was sent to photograph the deceased, and that the body had been stripped. He was taken aback to see the kid had no pubic hair. He was that young. The deputy floated through the event, I guess, without negative repercussions. Ultimately, I heard from three or four sources – people I knew from the department—that he was canned for stealing from dead people while working in the Identification Section. I was told that later he'd filed for divorce in order to remarry. Infuriated, his estranged wife brought in a bag of jewelry and dumped it on the sheriff's desk, saying that he had taken these valuables off cadavers while processing the scenes.

In committing these illegalities, one would wonder if the disposition of the cases had been changed. In some, the investigating detective might come to the conclusion that there was perhaps a motive of robbery and that the death might have occurred under different circumstances. As can be imagined, taking personal items of value from the scene of a death might seriously screw up the direction of an investigation. If family members reported that their loved one's valuables were missing, one can only speculate how this might send the investigator off in an entirely different direction.

THE MAYS OF AMERICA are from the Anglo-Norman family of De Maise (such it seems was the original spelling), and are the descendants of two knights, Eleaz and John De Maies, of the Demesne of Barfleur, Val de Saire, Normandy. In medieval times the streets of Barfleur were clogged with the comings and goings of dukes and kings and traders, and it was the biggest port in Normandy. In 1066, Eleaz and John De Maies, entered England in the "suite of William," and for valorous services at the battle of Hastings where, by royal charter, they were granted the manor known as King's Chase, afterwards Mayfield, in the County of Sussex. Today, Barfleur, 25 km east of Cherbourg, has a bronze plaque affixed to a cottage size granite flagstone at quayside commemorating where William the Conqueror's ship La Mora was built. And it was from Barfleur Harbor the little drakkar was sailed on this momentous voyage to conquer.

FROM: Descendants of JOHN MAY of Roxbury, Mass. 1640, 1878, 1978 (Second Edition)

In July1635, Capt. John May (1590–1655), from Mayfield, Sussex, sailed from England, in his little freighter *James*. He arrived in Massachusetts Bay the last week of September 1635. With him were wife Sarah Brewer-May (1590–1651) and their twin sons John (1629-1671) and Samuel (1629-1695).

I have meandered the streets of Mayfield, in Sussex, and visited the quaint little harbor of Barfleur. I believe it is from Eleaz and John DeMaise that I have descended.

CHAPTER FOUR

Learning the Ropes

THERE ARE A LOT OF McMullens in Pinellas County. Always have been. They were in this chunk of coastal real estate when it was Hillsborough County, even before that war between the north and south. There were McMullens that worked for the sheriff's office, some at the McMullen Feed Store in Largo. Dan McMullen was a lawyer, nice guy, a friend. If you're not a McMullen, you're probably linked to one through marriage. If you're a Booth or a Johnson or a Curry or a Mitchell there's a good chance you're related to one of those Scottish decedents. Pinellas is a *cousinie* kind of county. Everyone's related one way or another. There are cousins and uncles and aunts around here who don't even know each other. There's an old saying that you never talk *about* a McMullen. You talk to them.

I parked my car on the shady drive dissecting the McMullen family cemetery on Coachman Road, out east of Clearwater. Standing in the summer sun, taller than all other headstones—except Dan's—is the antediluvian monument of *Captain James P. McMullen (b.1823-d.1895), Army of the Confederacy.* History chronicles the four year conflict as the American Civil War, but Captain McMullen would have probably described it as the War of Northern Aggression. Bethel McMullen (b.1845-d.1940) and the Captain's graves were decorated with small Confederate flags on rounded wooden sticks punched down in the sandy soil.

Another headstone marked the burial plot for James McMullen Sr., American Revolutionary War soldier. In June 1999, his remains were moved here from Hickory Head, Brooks County, GA.

CARL McMULLEN (b.1925 – d.2013): Then there was Carl Ramage McMullen, a World War II paratrooper, a rodeo rider, a Florida Highway Trooper, and a deputy sheriff. His great-grandfather, Daniel McMullen, was one of seven brothers who moved to the Clearwater area in the 1850s from Georgia.

As I grow older, I am persuaded that there may be something to reincarnation, re-embodiment. I've read a lot of the books on the subject. In another life Carl must have been a skilled horseman and gun manipulator. There was nothing in his character suggesting he'd face down an outlaw in the middle of the street, and wait for the other guy to blink. He wasn't Matt Dillon or Hollywood or Louis L'Amour. As a lawman, he acted first, and come hell or high water, took the bad guy down by whatever means necessary.

On a June day in 1965, two armed miscreants held up a grocery store in Kenneth City and got away with several thousand dollars stuffed in a canvas traveling bag. Racing north on 49th Street they managed to make it as far as Ulmerton Road without being taken, even though two experienced deputies, John Hardman and Gary Smith, were in close pursuit. After turning east towards the Howard Franklin Bridge and the City of Tampa the robbers kicked it up to 90 m.p.h. Carl, riding alone, eased alongside the left rear panel of the bad guys' Ford Mustang, rolled down his driver's side window, rested his left arm on the window frame,

June 26 1965. Lieutenant Carl McMullen, who says 14 minutes after he got the call he had the captives. Deputy McMullen and gun used in capture. (Photo by Weaver Tripp) Reprinted with permission of The Tampa Bay Times. All Rights Reserved.

steadied his wrist on the spotlight, and fired two shots from his .38 S&W Combat Masterpiece across the hood of his cruiser. The second round hit the driver in the left shoulder.

The chase was over.

It was a remarkable feat particularly for someone right handed. There were a few lawmen I worked with that would have hooted and strutted and made a victory lap after such an accomplishment. But that wasn't Carl. He kept his ego in check. In his mind he was supposed to win. He was one of the good guys, not a talker, but a doer and a force to be reckoned with. He was a powerful mentor and I, along with other troops, learned from him a proper code of conduct.

In a fictional match up, I could see Carl knocking the snot out of Hulk Hogan, a guy at least three times his size—all show biz, muscle, and bluster. I'm not belittling the Hulkster, he's okay, but he's an entertainer, while Carl was quiet, determined and tenacious . . . you'd have to kill him to stop him. There's an old saying, an amateur plays for fun—a professional plays for keeps. I doubt that Carl or his kind could survive in today's world of mindless political correctness.

Incidentally, President Harry S. Truman is credited with explaining the doctrine of political correctness, saying that it was fostered by a delusional, illogical minority and promoted by the sick mainstream media, which holds the proposition that it is entirely possible to pick up a turd by the clean end.

IIIIIIIIIIIIIIIIIIIIIIIIIIIIIIIIIIIIIIIIIIIIIIIIIIIIIIIIIIIIIIIIIIIIIIIIIIII
"I was untested, as green as an Appalachian front tooth, and had yet to make an arrest."

IIIIIIIIIIIIIIIIIIIIIIIIIIIIIIIIIIIIIIIIIIIIIIIIIIIIIIIIIIIIIIIIIIIIIIIIIIII

My first encounter with Carl happened on a muggy summer night in a distressed, run-down neighborhood between Clearwater and

Largo. I was untested—as green as an Appalachian front tooth—and had yet to make an arrest.

A little after midnight, radio sent me on a noise complaint. A commotion was going on over on Crawford Avenue, a white sock and black brogan neighborhood. I was told how to get there and the name of the complainant. That seemed simple enough. I wanted to think, that because of my limited experience, Claude Oller, the old and crotchety radio operator, was careful not to send me out on anything too problematic.

That was not to be the case.

When I arrived an aggrieved father stood in the gravel road in his undershorts and bare feet, holding a pretty but grubby little wide eyed girl. It was hot and sticky and doors and windows along the street were open to catch some kind of relief. Swarms of enormous mosquitoes buzzed in noisy black clouds. Honkytonk music came blasting from the darkened shack close by. The complainant pointed, and explained "that bastard over there" was a mean, disruptive, drunk that instigated regular weekend disturbances.

I dutifully wrote down the complainant's name and phone number and, patting the little girl on the head, assured the aggrieved father I would solve his dilemma straightaway. With considerable bravado I strolled onto the troublemaker's rotted porch and heartily pounded on the decaying screen door. Rap, rap, rap! I was the law, I had a badge and by god there would be consequences if this agitator did not respect the peace and tranquility of his neighbors. Damn it, anyhow! He would cease and desist with his annoyance, forthwith. I was ticked off, puffed up and going to take care of the problem forthwith, and so forth, and …. well, you get the picture.

"Get the hell off my porch," the offender bellowed from inside the murky interior. I couldn't see anything, but the unpleasant whiff of fried onions, mangy dog, and other odd unrecognizable odors oozed out the screen door. "I know my rights! You can't arrest me without a warrant . . . and YOU can kiss my rosy red ass. Now get the hell off my property."

Where was he? No matter how many times I knocked or called his name he refused to show himself. I pressed my nose against the rusted screen and shaded my eyes. Nothing. The radio continued to blast. This was not good. Bamboozled, I meandered back to my cruiser, wondering what to do next. Should I call radio for advice, for help? I didn't know. Neighbors gathered in their front yards, speaking in hushed tones. They saw me as the Lone Ranger, a Pinellas County deputy sheriff was on the scene and by golly the problem would be resolved. I looked in the rear-view mirror and saw a sorry-eyed Barney Fife staring back. My bluff had been called. I sensed defeat.

It wasn't supposed to be this way.

Stalled there on my backside, feeling inadequate in my lofty new Stetson, I spotted a pair of parking lights idling slowly up the unlit street, coming in my direction. The car stopped close in behind my green and white. Out climbed my shift sergeant with a smoldering cigar clenched in his teeth. Carl McMullen wasn't a big man in the sense of being tall, but he was solid as a cinder block. Clad in white uniform shirt and tie, he wasn't particularly intimidating in appearance until you become aware of his square jaw and penetrating, intense eyes. He was not to be messed with. With no howdy or greeting of any kind, he asked, "Whatta ya got?"

I explained the dilemma and ended with, "I think he's drunk."

Carl asked, "Who is he?"

"His name's Charlie May."

"He related?"

"No!"

From the house, country singer George Jones was yowling *She Thinks I still Care.*

While Carl and I stood talking in the yard—me filling him in on the problem— Charlie completely miscalculated the moment. He thought that because we were out there in his yard chatting, that he had us over a barrel, that there was nothing we could do . . . or were going to do. But, I'd been with the department long enough to know there was absolutely no way in hell a Pinellas Deputy Sheriff was going to walk away from a situation without resolving the problem, one way or the other, come hell or high water.

Unexpectedly, over confident and over indulged, Charlie's shadowy figure jumped out of the darkness and into the doorway, stomping and whooping. He was banging around like a hog on hemp. Carl stepped up close to the door, took the cigar from his mouth and held it near his back pocket. "Charlie, turn off the radio and go to bed. Its past one o'clock. Knock off the racket or I'm gonna lock you up."

Displaying a broken row of snuff stained teeth, Charlie started up howling again, flailing his arms over his head and stomping loudly, one foot, then the other. He knew his rights. The guy had the I.Q. of a small salad bar. Plus, he was extremely intoxicated; he couldn't have found his ass with both hands.

With one lightning quick snatch, Carl punched through the rotted screen, clamped one paw around Charlie's windpipe and yanked him out on the porch. I was dumbfounded. So was Charlie. I'd never seen anything like that in my young life. Not even in the movies. Carl told me to go in and turn off Mr. May's radio. Warrantless, I followed the sound of Little Jimmy Dickens' singing *May The Bluebird Of Paradise Fly Up Your Nose* and turned off the white cracked plastic radio lodged in the window facing the street.

Stepping back out through the fragmented screen door, I watched Carl drag Mr. May with one hand across the grassless yard. Charlie's wide butt smoothed a path in the dirt, while his number thirteens raked matching tracks straight from the porch to the back door of my Dodge. Without looking, Carl said, "Gimme your cuffs." He expertly snapped them on the prisoner, opened the cruiser door and, as Charlie leaned over to voluntarily climb in, Carl kicked Big Mouth's dusty butt, driving his head against the door on the opposite side. Ker thump. Carl slammed the door and said, "Charge Mr. May with drunk and disorderly, make his bond $27."

Turning, he asked, "You sure he's not related?" He didn't grin or say anything else so I guess it was his way of saying *he's all yours, get moving.*

He sauntered back to his unmarked unit and with lights still out, faded around the corner, leaving me feeling thoroughly inadequate. I was raised with a willingness to accept responsibility so I worried if I had handled the situation properly? Should I have taken some kind of action—any action—before Carl got there? Before leaving, I got no suggestions or direction from him. He wasn't unfriendly but he sure wasn't warm and fuzzy either. He was all business.

My first encounter with Carl McMullen was awkward, yet in certain ways exhilarating. I'd get to know him a little better down the road. He was a lawman's lawman. I can't remember him as a sergeant, lieutenant, or captain ever speaking critically of any guys under his command.

As I drove north on Fort Harrison Avenue towards the county jail, Mr. May pulled himself up straight and wiped his runny nose on the back of one shackled paw.

We made eye contact in the rear-view mirror.

I asked, "You married Charlie?"

"Yeah."

"Where's your wife?"

"She tends bar at the Midway (tavern)."

"Why aren't you over at the Midway, instead of aggravating your neighbors?"

"It's cheaper to drink at home," he answered in a serious tone.

"Not tonight, it wasn't."

Then Charlie asked, "Sir, what's your name?"

I told him.

"May?" He perked up, sat up straight. "Hell, my name's May. You're not gonna put me in jail are ya? We got the same name fer Christ sake! We might be related."

"Don't think so, Charlie . . . I haven't met a May around here yet that I thought was worth a damn," said I with a good measure of disdain. So there, I sure told him.

I knew all about the Midway Tavern, located a few blocks over on Missouri Avenue. (It's now ABC Liquor.) Still riding with an FTO (Field Training Officer), I had gone along with other deputies on a fight call to the Midway. Reportedly, several combatants were involved in an ongoing fracas. As Oscar Underwood, George Kearns, and other deputies went through, I was instructed to stand inside the double doors and stay out of the way. The band shut down, the fight stopped, and the crowd grew silent. For a split second you could hear water dripping in the bar sink. At that same moment an extremely inebriated and scrawny granny, a cigarette hanging from her face, with a shot glass in one hand and a mug of something in the other, drilled me with a hard stare and bellowed, "Wellll, I'll be damned! I thought you had to be twenty-one years old to be a deputy sheriff!"

Another time, one of the Midway bartenders smacked a transgressor over the head with a bottle of apricot brandy. He was coming across the bar with an open citrus knife after Tommy, a former boxer. The bottle shattered. When I arrested the incapacitated chap I had to resist licking my fingers.

Still a sergeant, Carl called via radio on another night, asked me to meet him in the parking lot of the Belleair Bar on Clearwater Largo Road. (C. Lacey Plumbing is now at that location.) He needed my traffic citation book. When I got there Carl had changed his mind about writing a ticket and arrested all four men in the car. He didn't explain. I didn't ask. He placed the driver and two others in his unmarked unit, told me to handcuff the fourth guy and follow him to the county jail. My guy was enormous, the biggest of the four. Carl said loud enough for the big guy to hear from the back seat, "If he gives you any trouble just knock the hell outta him with your nightstick."

The jail was either being built or remodeled, I can't remember. Heavy two-by-twelve planks provided the walkway up to the jail's Ft. Harrison Avenue entrance. Carl was ahead of me with his three arrestees while I tagged along behind with mine. Up to that point he'd been a creampuff. As we reached the door he stopped. I placed my hand in the middle of his back and said, "C'mon, let's go." He planted both feet, balled up his fists and declared, "By gawd, I aint' goin' in 'er." Carl turned. I thought he was simply looking to see what was going on. But he reached around the man, handed me my citation book and in the same movement slapped the man with an open hand. POW! The hit was louder than the discharge of a .357. The fellow dropped to the concrete like a bag of wet cow poop. Carl snatched up the body and threw it through the double doors as though tossing a hay bale. He calmly stepped over the wadded figure and went behind the booking counter.

Wobbling, the guy sat up, and took a moment to focus. The left half of his face was flaming red. His one bloodshot eye looked like a piss hole in an Indian blanket. Hoarsely, he asked, "Which one of you sons a'bitches hit me?" I pointed, "He did." Carl stopped writing, looked up and said, "Hold on. I'll be with you in a minute."

The guy nearly knocked down two jailers and a hallway door to get in to the cell area.

Riots began in the Watts neighborhood of Los Angeles in August 1965. The five-day insurrection resulted in 34 deaths, 1,032 injuries, 3,438 arrests, and over $40 million in property damage.

Thinking ahead, Sheriff Genung, realizing civil unrest would eventually come to us, and he decided to make early preparation for the inevitable. He obtained surplus 18-inch WWI bayonets which were adapted to the department's pump shotguns. Always the stickler for dress, he wanted his uniform deputies to look flawless with long sleeved white shirts, green ties, and green pants with gray stripes. Still, he knew the Stetson would be inappropriate head gear for riot control. He opted to get the public used to seeing his men in different lids; subsequently in late 1965 he changed the Stetson to a heavy plastic crash helmet.

That December, pictures appeared in local newspapers with articles that read: *SHERIFF'S OFFICE GETS NEW IMAGE WITH CRASH HELMETS TO REPLACE THE CLASSIC STETSON.* Sheriff Don Genung said the primary purpose was for safety in pursuit driving. The helmets cost about $19 each, and the old Stetsons would be issued to jailers. Forty-five deputies were fitted out with the new headgear.

"New Look for Sheriff's Deputies Reads The St Petersburg Times": Standing: Dayrl May in Stetson, Sheriff Don Genung and Captain Carl McMullen. Seated: Gary Stevenson "center", and don't worry about "Mr. Shades" (grin), and Frank Coleman. Dec 31 1965. Staff Photo by Frances Brush

Next, the Sheriff sent out a department memo that the helmet would be worn both outside and inside the cruisers, during interviews, and answering complaints—you name it, at all times. There would be absolutely no exception. He was emphatic, wanting the general public to get used to seeing his deputies in that gawd awful head gear. The troops, including sergeants, lieutenants, and captains, hated the damned things, but that's what

Genung wanted and that's what Genung got. He was the boss, he signed the paychecks.

But, we all took chances, slipping the helmet off when we got out on the road. But, we kept it within arm's reach at all times. Then one gorgeous sunny morning at the S.O. airport office, a deputy—we'll call him K.P.—came down the steps with his briefcase, clip board, shotgun, and helmet in hand to start the dayshift. He went to his assigned cruiser, placed the helmet on the roof of his green and white, dropped his briefcase on the front seat and shoved the shotgun in the zippered sheath along the front seat. He got his clipboard, walked around the cruiser to check for any new dings and dents, got behind the wheel, recorded the mileage as required and drove away from the airport.

There was very little traffic on Roosevelt Blvd., then a two lane road, so K.P. kicked it as he turned right and headed towards Largo. What he didn't hear or realize was that his brand spanking new white plastic helmet rolled off the top of his vehicle and bounced like a soccer ball across the weeded shoulder, and came to rest in a shallow ditch.

K.P. keyed the mic, "Zone Two, I'll be 10-8." He was now officially on duty and ready if duty called, but, for the moment, unaware he was helmetless.

Headed for the office that morning, Carl McMullen, then a lieutenant in uniform, spotted the shiny *chapeau* shimmering at the bottom of the ditch. Retrieving the slightly scratched and soiled object, he saw that the initials on the inside were K.P., the errant deputy. When he reached his desk, Carl picked up the phone and called radio, requesting that the deputy in question return to the office and see him as soon as possible.

Wondering what it was all about, K.P. returned to the airport, parked his car and looked for his helmet. Dang! He had no clue where the dang thing was. So, he went to his locker, took off his gun belt and made his way to the Carl's office.

"You wanted to see me lieutenant?"

"Yeah. How ya doin'?"

"I'm fine lieutenant."

"Where's your leather?"

"In my locker. I thought while I was here I'd do some quick paper-work and take yesterday's field interrogation reports to the detective division."

The lieutenant reached down, picked the helmet off the floor, and placed it on his desk and looked at Deputy K.P. "Have any idea how your helmet ended up in the ditch over by the sandwich shop on Roosevelt?"

"No sir."

"I don't either. But the next time I find your helmet in a ditch your (expletive) head had better be in it!"

Deputy Daryl May
(art work by George Miller)

CHAPTER FIVE

The Judge & The Rooster

RIGHT IN THE MIDDLE of my night shift radio called, said there was a disturbance going on at an all-night laundromat on East Bay Drive, just west of Belcher Road. I knew the place. Gary Stevenson, in the float car, showed up in case I needed assistance. We got there about the same time.

At the rear of the neon-lighted coin laundry we spotted this pint-sized dirt bag, who might have weighed in at 140 pounds if he had a pocket full of nails. He was bopping around like a skinny necked rooster on a hot plate, punching it out with a fat babe three times his size. Clad in a ripped Cypress Garden t-shirt, filthy khaki shorts, and flip-flops, he was bleeding profusely at the nose and on the knuckles. His beady eyes were as black as his hair . . . and his feet about the same color. It also struck me that his eyes were extremely close together. To me, that's relevant. I never trust anybody whose eyes are squashed up against their nose. This squirrely little dude looked like a shifty eyed, grungy footed bandy rooster.

Each time the babe whacked Rooster up 'side the head she'd do a hard squint, and bite her lower lip with vicious intensity. All her shots were connecting. She was dishing out the better thumps. But, little guys can be a handful. We were cautious. He could be packin' and willing to do harm. Gary goes down the washing machine isle and I go down the dryer side. I looked over at my partner. He looks back. Nothing needed to be said. We both knew what each other was thinking and what the other would do. We cornered knob-by-knees between the folding table and the Coke machine.

First off we assumed the lady owned the place. She was out of breath but, holding her own in the struggle, fighting as though the terrain belonged to her. Each had worked up a sticky sweat which told me they'd probably been going at it all during the wash, rinse, and spin cycles. We wrenched them apart.

I tried to get at least five nights out of a white uniform shirt, so I was careful not to get too close or wrestle with either combatant. Rosende's Laundry in Largo charged 27 cents to wash and starch a shirt. With a little luck, I could get through a midnight shift for a buck-eight.

Anyhow, while Gary pinned the flyweight to the wall with his nightstick, I ascertained from Miss Piggy that the slugfest was actually a lovers' tiff.

Well, bless their hearts.

Rooster promised to behave but the second he was unfastened from the wall, and turned loose, he cranked up again, cussing and swinging at us, trying to get to girlfriend. Rather than knock the dog poop outta this feisty little dork we resorted to handcuffs, then pulled him, struggling, out through the sliding glass doors to my cruiser, curbside. During all this, the girlfriend commenced working up a head of steam, not wanting lover boy to be incarcerated. Too late. Well, the long and the short of it is that I hauled Rooster to the hoosegow, charged him with drunk and disorderly and set his bond at the very minimum, hoping he'd forfeit and not show up later for court.

It didn't work. A few days later in Justice of the Peace Court, Judge Joe Clark listened attentively as Rooster, now looking presentable, and Miss Piggy, wearing a faded Frederick's of Hollywood mini-skirt and red ankle-strap spikes, explained in great detail they were simply doing their laundry, minding their own affairs—yes, they'd had a couple beers and yes they were having a bit of a lovers' quarrel when these two deputies . . . she pointed . . . arrived and, for absolutely no *justifiable* reason, busted Rooster's lip, blacked his eye, and put him in jail. She insisted that it was the cops that had roughed up lover boy. To add insult to injury, someone ripped-off their laundry and full box of Tide. They'd been victimized all around.

I'd been stuck a few times with being bailiff in Clark's court. The chore entailed picking up prisoners at the jail, hauling them to court, and then making sure order ruled during sessions. When the judge entered the courtroom the bailiff called out a prescribe pronouncement that went something like this:

All rise. Justice of the Peace Court District Three is now in session. The Honorable Joseph Clark will be presiding. There will be no talking or smoking in the courtroom. Please come forward when your name is called . . . and do not lean on the judge's bench. Be seated.

No pleases and no thank-you.

On this day, however, I was in Clark's Safety Harbor court as an arresting officer. When Rooster's name was called, Clark, who had a lifelong love affair with his own voice, launched into a spiel about how responsible citizens should behave themselves, respect the law, the peace and tranquility of a neighborhood, or a business, zippity-blah, blah. Under oath, I gave detailed testimony. The defendant's small size was the deciding factor. The judge, I think, found it hard to believe Rooster was that much trouble for two good sized deputies. Clark turned him loose and gave back his 27-bucks.

Soon after, I got a call from J. Edger Hoover's Tampa FBI office. The special agent said he was obliged to look into a complaint filed against me for violating Rooster's civil rights, that it was necessary to conduct a "routine" interview. When could he and a colleague meet with me at our airport office?

In order to back up each other and verify testimony, federal agents always conducted interviews in pairs. Who was he bullshitting? This was definitely not a routine matter but something I judged as pretty serious. I told the agent I'd speak with my lieutenant and get back to him after I finished the midnight shift. The agent acceded.

Carl McMullen said, "Tell 'em to piss off."

"Can I do that?"

"Hell yes. You don't have to talk to those (*expletives*)."

Wow! Too cool! I got on the phone and relayed those sentiments to the agent. That was the last I heard of it.

Months later, during another midnight shift, radio called me, said there was a drunk and disorderly person "at that laundromat over there on East Bay." He asked, "Isn't that the same place you went to once before?" I gave a resounding, "10–4." As I pulled up in front of the lighted laundromat, Deputy Stevenson showed up out of curiosity. It couldn't possibly be Rooster. Sure enough, it was him and Miss Piggy going at it again, busting each other's chops. Rooster was nastier, drunker, and more belligerent than before. Miss P. was holding her own but crying spit. This time it was a bang up donnybrook. Without so much as a "howya doin'" we loaded Rooster in the cruiser, but on the way outside he fell down several times, and *tripped* against the cruiser, *bumping* his bean more than once.

I came on the air, "Zone 2, I'm 10–15 (got a prisoner) one time, and 10–51 (on my way to) the county jail."

Sergeant Tommy "Catfish" Johnson radioed, "Is that the same drunk you arrested at that laundromat once before?"

"10–4."

He asked, "Is he as bad (drunk and disorderly) as last time."

"Worse."

"Didn't (Judge) Clark turn him loose the first go around?"

"That's a 10–4."

"Before you book the guy, take him by Judge Clark's house . . . over on Belleair Road . . . 10–4?"

"It's goin' on 3:30. Ya think that's a good idea?"

"I do!" Catfish answered, "Take him to Clark's, get him outta bed. I'll meet you there."

So off I went with a cuffed Rooster in the back seat, and Deputy Gary Stevenson following behind in his cruiser. My prisoner had grown quiet. I was hoping he was not sobering up.

Rooster asked, "Where we going?"

"I'm taking your skinny butt to jail, but on the way I wanna stop off and see somebody." I asked, "Tell me something, Skippy, how come you and your fiancé fight all the time?"

Rooster replied, "She ain't my fiancée no more."

"No? Why's that?"

Pulling into Judge Clark's driveway, he answered. "Fat girls and mopeds are alike. They're fun to ride until a friend sees you." He erupted in thick, phlegmy tobacco choked laughter that came out sounding like extended croaks. That's an old joke today but it was the first time I'd heard it. It was funny and I laughed along with him. I've remembered that one liner ever since.

In his twenties, Rooster had a wry sense of humor, and would probably go through life getting a lot of butt-kickings. Miss Piggy just couldn't help herself, she loved the little booger. Ladies love outlaws.

Anyhow, the judge, rousted from his bed, stepped outside in his slippers and robe. Following was Mrs. Mary Clark, the judge's wife and proficient office secretary. She was a great lady, a real gem, who kept Clark and his office running.

Had he been sober, Rooster just might have recognized the Right Honorable Judge Joseph Clark . . . or maybe if His Honor had been dressed in somber, black judicial garb instead of a ratty blue chenille robe. But, alas, when Clark leaned in close to the open window, Rooster's greeting was loud and profane, commenting on the judge's chunky stature and so-on and so-forth. Thus it was the one and only time, during my law enforcement career, that I got a lawn conviction, in the dark, under a palm tree, and before the prisoner reached the jail.

Incidentally, Lt. McMullen asked and I was pleased to inform him, I'd not heard anything further from the Federal Bureau of Investigation.

Carl McMullen was unpretentious and exuded a powerful, controlled no-nonsense demeanor. He could be persuasive but was a man of limited words. He smiled easily, but I can't remember him ever laughing out loud, a belly laugh. He didn't hand out "atta boys" but you knew when he was pleased or displeased. Few knew he could play a decent guitar and sing a ballad in a clear and relaxed baritone voice. He was my sergeant when I signed on and he eventually made captain. Unhappy with Sheriff Genung rotating supervisors . . . called them lateral transfers . . . Carl declined to become captain of the jail and left the sheriff's department to go to work for his buddy Chick Smith, owner of the Ford Dealership in *"Sparkling Downtown Clearwater."*

CHAPTER SIX

Roy M. Speer, Attorney

THE SIZEABLE OBITUARY FOR Roy Merrill Speer said that as co-founder of the television giant Home Shopping Network, a company based in Pinellas County, he had become, according to Forbes 400, one of the wealthiest Americans. He was from Key West, attended Stetson Law School, and got himself appointed as an assistant state attorney for a couple years. He was a big man with a giant ego. He was bright and abrasive and a bit of a bully. "I don't like people," he told the Washington Post, "I like machines. Machines don't call in sick. Machines don't form unions. Machines don't file (law) suits."

For a while in the 1960s, he was a heavy player in Florida's political process, but said, "I don't have the personality for politics. You have to be conciliatory."

One Saturday evening, while working the 3-to-11shift in a county area that butted up against the city limits of St. Petersburg, dispatch (radio) called me to say Car 11 (that was the Sheriff) wanted me (Zone 1) to meet up with a Mr. Speer at the St. Petersburg Yacht Club. I was to provide an official escort for the man and his two-car entourage and take them to the Derby Lane Dog Track way out on Gandy Boulevard.

||||||||||||||||||||||||||||||||||||||||||||||||||||||||||||||||||||||||
Without so much as a "shit howdy," he waved towards two black Lincolns and admonished me for being late. I had kept his guest, the honorable C. Farris Bryant, Governor of this great state of Florida, waiting."

||||||||||||||||||||||||||||||||||||||||||||||||||||||||||||||||||||||||

Still, a bit green (experience wise), my confidence at times was a little shaky. Who the heck is Roy Speer? Pulling into the yacht club, I was instantly waylaid by an enormous man with the disposition of a Luftwaffe Commander. He lacked only a uniform, a Knight's Cross of Iron, and a silver baton. Without so much as a "shit howdy," he waved towards two black Lincolns and admonished me for being late.

He quickly pointed out that I had kept his guest, the honorable C. Farris Bryant, Governor of the Great State of Florida, and his staff, *and* the mayor of St. Petersburg, waiting. He informed me that I was to escort his distinguished entourage to the Gandy dog track for a political gathering of significant importance. And because of my tardiness they were now late. To save time Speer, told me we would take a short cut through Snell Island, an old and affluent upper-class neighborhood. He snapped that he would be driving the first car with the governor. It was important that I should know that.

I was staggered with this critically important assignment. My young mind was thinking, *"I am in deep trouble!"* I had never been assigned anything this important before. Why me? All at once I was responsible for getting the governor of Florida someplace important, and in a hurry. We're late, and I don't have a clue where Snell Isle is. I sure as heck didn't want to ask Genghis Kahn. Recognizing the vacant look on my face, Speer pointed, "… just go north on 4th Street, then turn east on 22nd Avenue. We'll take Snell Island Boulevard then hook up with (such and such a street) blah, blah, blah." My brain switched to a low hum. I could see Speer's lips moving, yet there was nothing but garbled noises coming from the front of his face, like static from an AM radio. I jerked out of it when he clapped his hands, and ordered, "Okay. Let's go!" I rushed to my cruiser. He snapped a wave for me to take the lead.

Looking straight ahead, and tooling along 4th Street, I was astonished to look over and see Speer, with the governor sitting on the passenger side and the window down. He screamed, "Turn on your (expletive) red light and get a (expletive) move on, for

Christ's sake!" All heads in both limos stared in my direction with the exception of Governor Bryant who was flexing his jaw muscles and glaring at the headliner.

Seconds after crossing the Snell Island Bridge, I found myself heading down a dark tree lined street. We dead-ended. Holy crap! Slowing to a stop, I turn off my overhead flasher and tried to figure out how to turn around without backing into the governor's limousine. Roy Speer was right on my back bumper. As previously mentioned, in those days, police cruisers had no air conditioning. My shirt collar was damp and tightening. I was on the verge of hyperventilating.

A sputtering, red-faced Speer appeared at my open window. He shouted, "Dammit all, follow me, and I'll get us the hell outta here. Just before we get to Gandy, I'll flash my lights, and then you take the lead and get us to the main entrance of the main building. You do know where Derby Lane is, don'tcha? *And turn on your (expletive) red light, damnit!*" Back then a cruiser's red light looked like (and was called) a gumball machine.

With much seesawing back and forth, we disentangled our vehicles and got headed back in the direction we had come. Off we went once again. I struggled to keep up as the two black cars zoomed around curves and along darkened streets, my rotating red gumball reflected off the trees, houses, and passing cars. I was lighting up the neighborhood. Finally, nearing Gandy Boulevard, Speer slammed on his brakes, flashed his headlights, and frantically waved me ahead. As I eased by, I got zombie stares from everyone in both cars. Stressed out, anxious and intimidated, I stared straight ahead and floored it. Mighty engines roared. With much fanfare, I led the way through the enormous parking lot jam-packed with traffic. Failing to slow down, I shot into the portico like Richard Petty's greased pig. My left front tire banged loudly over the curb. Speer, following too close, repeated the blunder. We thumped and scraped to a stop as both species of formally dressed dignitaries jumped to safety. Speer ran at me, yelling, "Don't get out!" He shoved a $50 bill through the window and hissed, "The governor said you should buy a (expletive) map and take some (expletive) driving lessons. You better get outta here before he changes his mind and wants his money back."

In retrospect I think the Derby Lane arrival was, for me at least, notable and exciting. We didn't hit anybody. And, fifty dollars was a heck of a lot of money. I couldn't wait to get home and tell Marilyn. From my perspective, the evening had been memorable.

CHAPTER SEVEN

Sheriff Don Genung

"To be trusted is a greater compliment than to be loved." —George MacDonald

WITH THE EXCEPTION OF my dad, Al May, I probably admired Sheriff Genung more than any man I've known in this life. For 17 years he remained the elected sheriff until *he* decided it was time to retire. A highly respected and popular Democrat in a Republican County, I don't believe he suffered ego. There was no question in his mind that he was the boss. He was fond of saying, Pinellas has one sheriff and you're looking at him. He was easy going but no pushover, and stood head and shoulders above the run-of-the-mill Florida sheriffs and politicos of that era. He was sophisticated, an open-minded thinker, an innovator, and a humanitarian. His word and hand shake could be taken to the bank. If he told you he was going to shoot you at 9:00 P.M. you best consult a funeral director before the six o'clock news.

I don't remember him bad-mouthing anyone because of political differences or holding a grudge. As one of only two Democrats in the county he worked with Republicans and he got things done. He could do business with anyone as long as they were honorable and sincere. When it came time to do his job—the job he'd taken an oath to do—he was focused with zero tolerance.

Summoned to the Kennedy family's Palm Beach compound by Jack Kennedy, the new president, Genung was urged to run for Congress. He needed men of the sheriff's caliber in Washington. Content at being sheriff, he declined the president's request—twice.

Genung had large hands and dark eyes resembling crooner Tony Martin, possessed a great sense of humor, and was fair-minded and compassionate.

He probably had good reason to fire me a couple times. During the writing of this book, I was chatting with my son Scott, a Pinellas County Sheriff's detective, with 20–plus years under his belt. He was making some comments about Internal Affairs, the unit that investigates problems within the department.

I told Scott, "I'm glad we didn't have Internal Affairs when I was with the sheriff's office."

Scott said, "Dad, you're the reason we have Internal Affairs!"

During the years I worked for Genung, I managed to damage six county vehicles. He hailed me one morning, shouting down the hallway, "Son, did you break one of my cruisers?"

"I did, boss."

"You hurt?"

"No, sir . . . not a scratch."

He was alluding to my "fender bender" a couple nights before when my cruiser ended-up, upside-down in a ditch near the Kapok Tree Restaurant on a Christmas Eve.

I was working Zone 3 & 4 when four senior citizens, their backs to traffic, went strolling in the middle of McMullen-Booth Road, then a two lane blacktop. Just in the nick of time, I flipped on my high beams, saw them, locked up the brakes, missed, skidded, spun 180, bumped the road-side turf and did a slow roll-over, *plunk!,* into the ditch, up-side down. Shotgun, clipboard, briefcase, flashlight, nightstick, and a couple years' worth of accumulated loose crap knocked about my head like debris in a dust devil, settling on the headliner that was now the floor. A strong odor of gas filled the interior as the vehicle rocked and came to rest. There were no seatbelts in those days, and my six-foot frame was wadded up like a spitball, up under the dash. Fearing an electrical spark from the radio might ignite the fumes, I fumbled around in the dark to turn it off. Rolling the window down—in this case up—I began wiggling out, feet first. All at once people started tugging on my legs. It was the jay-walkers to the rescue. I kicked and cussed for them to back-off!

It was too dark and too far to walk to the Kapok Restaurant to make a phone call. The "gumball" on the roof had caved-in the car's top. Despite the tight squeeze, I crawling back inside, groped again in the darkness, and turned the radio back on. Triggering the mike, I informed George Lusby, filling in as radio operator, that my cruiser was on its top a little south of the Kapok Tree.

"I'm okay, George. I'm not hurt." Lusby advised he would inform Buddy Young, our shift sergeant, and notify FHP, and as an afterthought, he said, "Don't go anywhere."

I jammed the mike button, "How the hell do you think I'm gonna go someplace, Lusby?"

Chief Deputy Bill Roberts told the story about Genung, as a Clearwater patrolman, arresting a knee-walkin', ankle-draggin' drunk on North Greenwood Avenue. The man had seriously soiled himself. Genung hauled Mr. Pooper to the city jail in the trunk of his cruiser. But before booking the poor soul, he hosed him down in the station's parking lot. I suppose it was situations like that, by which the sheriff could identify with the everyday calamities that happened to his guys, his deputies out on the street.

Early years with the S.O. were not easy. Even though I loved the job, trying to support a family on a deputy's pay was tough. Starting salary was something like $97.00 a week and we got paid once a month. My wife, Marilyn, worked for peanuts at the First National Bank, downtown Clearwater. Years later, the bank was still paying her peanuts as a supervisor. We had one car. Some early mornings, Marilyn walked (and sometimes carried) our little girls, Perri and Wendy, to a neighborhood babysitter before catching the bus downtown. To try and make ends meet, I got permission to work a part time job. I'd get off the midnight shift at seven in the morning, and be at Bob Smart's Town & Country Market, on Gulf to Bay, at eight. I'd knock off at two in the afternoon, go home, sleep until ten and be back to work at the S.O. in time to get in uniform and get out on patrol at eleven that night. During day shifts, I got off at three in the afternoon, made it to Town & Country by four and worked until the nine o'clock closing. Although it seemed an endless grind Marilyn and I were young, healthy, and happy to be making it on our own.

I never dreamed that one day I'd be paid $2,000 and expenses for a forty-five minute show, entertaining six-hundred captains of industry at the Grand National Water Foul Hunt in Cambridge, Maryland. Thanks to Doc Smith, it happened two years in a row.

I chanced to overhear Captain Herman Vincent comment to no one in particular that the sheriff was not asking for the usual 10% salary raise in the upcoming budget. Instead, he would ask for 5%. That was hard for me to fathom, he always got what he wanted— budget wise—from the county administrator and commissioners. A lot of us were bustin' our humps trying to make it from paycheck to paycheck. I asked Vincent for permission to go talk to the sheriff. He chuckled, "Sure go ahead, be my guest," scoffing at my naiveté, judging me ignorant of departmental protocol. Being a low guy on the department totem pole, he probably thought I would get my come-uppance by just talking to *The High Sheriff* about budget matters that I didn't understand and were really none of my business. Vincent was probably right. But, in this case, ignorance was bliss . . . I was thinking, nothing ventured; nothing gained.

After finishing the shift and driving from the airport in to Clearwater, I got a big smile from Florence, the sheriff's executive secretary (and wife). She was a grand lady, and as much a gentlewoman as the sheriff was a gentleman. Old Henry Anglin, the sheriff's gofer, always hanging around in the front office, gave me a friendly wave.

"You think the sheriff could give me a few minutes?" I asked. She opened the sheriff's door and said, "Don, Daryl would like to talk to you for a minute." He called out, "Sure. Get in here. What is it?" Blissfully ignorant, yet calm and confident, and standing with Stetson in hand, I told him of my concerns. After some discussion, he stood, grabbed a two-inch thick binder, threw it down on his desk, thud!, and said this year's budget would exceed three million dollars. "That's a lot of money! I can't give you a raise without giving everybody else a raise, damn it!"

"I know that boss, but what have you got to lose by asking for ten percent? If you don't get it, at least you tried." He cooled off, "Well, maybe I could use yours and a couple other deputies' salaries to make a case for ten percent." He didn't apologize but shook my hand and said, "Get outta here and let me get back to work."

After the budget was approved, Captain Vincent told me the sheriff had gotten the 10% salary increase. His only comment was to ask, "What the heck did you say to him?"

Old Henry Anglin, always on top of department gossip and hearsay, was the single uniform deputy assigned a *take-home* cruiser— Car 54 ("Where Are You?"). Back then, only detectives were lucky enough to be permanently assigned vehicles. I don't know what Henry had on the boss but he often threatened to marry the Genung's elderly mother. Then he'd be "running this outfit." It amused the boss.

Days later, Henry, a retired St. Petersburg bus driver, who spoke with a thick syrupy southern accent, cornered me and said, "Ya know, boy, you got the sheriff into some pretty serious trouble when you hit him up for that raise?"

"Really!? How's that, Henry?"

"After you left, Florence went in his office and said, 'Don, you shouldn't have talked to that boy that way! He's concerned about his family.'"

Chuckling, Henry said, "She gave him a reeeeal good going over." Then he said, "By the way, thanks for the raise."

RIOTS: Under Florida law, the sheriff derives authority from the Constitution of the State of Florida. It is the sheriff's duty to enforce both the Florida Constitution and Florida statutes. The most recognizable aspect of the sheriff's duties is that *the sheriff is the chief law enforcement officer of the county*—chapter 30 specifically designates the sheriff as the *"conservator of the peace in the county,"* to provide for the security, safety, and well-being of its citizens. He is also keeper of the county jail.

In August 1968, three months after St. Petersburg city sanitation workers went on strike, mounting tensions quickly turned to violence after some city cops beat the blazes outta Joseph Waller, later known as Omali Yeshitela. During the strike City Manager Lynn Andrews handled negotiations with the demonstrators and for a while everything pointed to a peaceful solution. Then in an instant everything went down the toilet and up in smoke.

On the eve of the riots, Genung called me at home. He said, "Damn it, the governor just called. He wants to know what's going on in St. Pete." Governor Claude Kirk, a blustery, heavy boozer and former U.S. Marine, demanded details. The governor tried calling Chief Harold Smith, but no one knew much of anything, or details of what was going on inside the city. All the governor knew was that a riot had broken out (or was about to), that some fires, looting, vandalism, and random shootings were taking place in a large area around 4th Street and 16th Avenue South.

Genung said, "Son, get down there, find Smith, see what's going on. Don Starr, with the Times, just called me and said Mel Coleman's down on the south side walking around with a Thompson submachine gun on his hip. See what that's all about." Coleman, formerly a lieutenant in St. Pete's vice squad, was now back in uniform, a good guy and a take charge individual. I liked him. He would become police chief of Winter Park and later appointed sheriff in Orange County (Orlando) by the governor. I would see Coleman's cockiness (the Coleman Strut) first hand, when I made it out on the streets the following night. Tactically, a submachine gun has little value in a riot except to aggravate adversaries.

I hurriedly drove from my home in Clearwater down to the St. Petersburg police station. The building was unusually dark, nearly deserted, like a commercial shop closed for the night. Few people were outside. Inside, I ask an over-weight sergeant manning the information desk where I could find Chief Smith's office. Scarcely looking up, he nonchalantly pointed towards the stairs, told me there was a door "up there" with Smith's name on it.

I knocked and found the chief alone in his office, parked behind a big uncluttered desk. His demeanor conveyed bewilderment. He was uninformed, out of touch, and said he didn't know anything at the moment, that he was waiting for Lieutenant Coleman to call in a report. Dumbfounded, I stood wondering why he, instead of Coleman, wasn't out on the streets managing the troops, quelling the insurrection. He seemed a bit dim, not up to speed. Bless his heart. Sorry, maybe that was an unkind judgment call. I'd had dinner, maybe he hadn't. Maybe he'd had a stressful day and needed a NoDoz. I'd brought coffee with me and felt alert, on my toes. Maybe as the sheriff's emissary, I was expecting too much, too soon.

Outside I located a pay phone, and called the Sheriff at home, told him if one could judge the so-called riot by the lack of activity at the police station (and what I'd just heard from the Chief Smith) there was nothing going on except a rowdy bingo game down on 22nd Avenue South; not the beginnings of a full-fledged, all-out riot. The sheriff also expressed concern Smith wasn't on the street with his people.

The uprising lasted four long days and caused major destruction. Citizens were injured and 150 deputies and policemen entered the rioting areas with orders to "shoot to kill" looters. Damages reached an estimated $150,000 and 335 fires had been set during the unrest.

To make a long story short (too late?), that first night the prover-bial doo-doo had hit the propeller, and things got worse. Genung quickly mustered the department's riot squad and our guys hit the streets armed with 18-inch WWI bayonets affixed to 12-gauge pump shotguns. Thanks to the sheriff, Captains Carl McMullen and Herman Vincent, Lieutenants George McNally and Lou Kubler, and a multitude of St. Pete cops and Florida Troopers peace was restored in due time.

As a side note, for the first time in my cop career I was (or thought I was) a target. Checking a dark alley for suspects, Will Stiegler and I got a shock, a real eye opener. We recognized the spit of a small caliber gun discharged in the darkness. Even more recognizable was the angry buzz of a passing slug. We knew the direction from which the gun was fired but were unable to locate the shooter. It was a hard hat area. Can you have any more fun than that?

ROLAND & PIERRE'S: At the close of one of those long hot gru-eling riot days and nights on the streets, walking neighborhoods and back alleys, Det. Leigh McEachern, with St. Pete Vice, declared he was "going to have a decent meal tonight." Around sundown we took ourselves far north of the unrest and sat at a roundtable at Roland & Pierre's, a fashionable and expensive restaurant that catered to high rollers and the city's elite. Leigh, Mel Coleman and Mickey Romanello and other S.P.P.D. detectives wallowed in steaks and martinis. Still on duty, I felt obliged (nay, compelled), to order only a burger, fries and milk. Sitting there, sipping my glass-of-moo, I secretly craved two—maybe three—very dry vodka marti-nis. As we feasted, who should walk in but Sheriff Genung, Chief Deputy Bill Roberts, and some other high ranking officials? Ah ha, a shot of pride hit me due to my choice of meal. My boss, the High Sheriff, would certainly approve that I, one of his finest, who, out of all these other cops, was strong-willed, conscientious and ded-icated to the job. Genung, as was his practice, glad-handed every-one, complementing us for our labors on the streets, slapped me on the back. "You looked good out there today, son." Then, much to my chagrin, he picked up the tab for the entire table, telling us,

MARIJUANA IN BRICK FORM

CLEARWATER — Possession of bricks can be a crime if they are made of marijuana. Sheriff Don Genung (right) holds one of six compressed marijuana bricks seized when three of his deputies arrested Charles Mike Chapman, 17, and Robin Gale Steelman, 16, both of Tampa, and charged them with possession of marijuana. The Sheriff said this was the first time such bricks had been found in Pinellas County and they are believed to have been professionally made in Mexico or Central America. Shown examining the evidence are (left to right) detectives Daryl May and Frank Holloway, arresting officers; Lt. George McNally, in charge of vice investigations and Pinellas-Pasco State Attorney James T. Russell.

Credit The Sheriff's Star – 1970

"Thanks for the good work fellas. Enjoy." It was too late for me to order that martini, although I wanted, no, needed a double, straight up.

BOB PRINE'S STEAKHOUSE: Another time, Detective Warren McNeely and I were watching from Prine's 9th floor restaurant while Frank Holloway sat on the hood of his Corvette, waiting to make an undercover drug buy at the gas station, below and across the street. It was McNeely's idea. The restaurant was nearly empty and we had a clear view of Holloway from a window. Owner Bob Prine leaned on our table, complaining that he'd donated money to the sheriff's last two campaigns but that he hadn't bothered to keep in touch. "It's been months since he's come by my place or even called."

"I'd call him if I were you," was my response. As Prine continued to grumble, I looked over his shoulder and—low and behold! Who was stepping off the elevator? It was the Sheriff and Florence. They walked into the lounge and sat at the bar. Holy crap!

"Aw gawd, how do we explain this?"

The sheriff hailed us, "Get over here. Florence and I wanna buy you guys a drink." We said we already had drinks—but thanks—and were reluctant to tell him why we were there, on duty, drinking. He insisted. While I manned the window, McNeely stepped over and quietly fessed up that we were watching Holloway . . . that he was about to make a drug buy down on the street.

The sheriff said, "Why didn't you say so?" He sent drinks to our table.

I don't remember if the drug buy went down. Holloway wasn't wearing a wire, and said he spotted the sheriff, in his black four-door Chrysler with twin spotlights, but didn't know how to warn us, to give us a heads up.

(L-R) Deputy Warren King and me. Aftermath of high-speed chase in Seminole area. Pictured is one of several holes in car, results of a 12-guage pumpkin ball from my shotgun. Slug in my hand was found in the vehicle's trunk. (Photo courtesy of Dep. Mike Sharp)

The Marble

LIEUTENANT J. T. WAS A nice guy, but, I thought, he had a lot of dead air between the ears. Someone said they thought booze was a factor. He was one of those guys, always juggling several projects at the same time. Rarely did anything get finished. And if the job was finished, it was always half-assed or late. When asked if such-and-such a task was wrapped-up, he'd say "it's still in the works," he'd have "it" finished just as soon as he got that other job done for the sheriff, or the captain, or . . . do-dah, do-dah. He saw himself as the ultimate schmoozer. Somebody must have spiked his Pablum. There was always a jangle of keys hanging from his uniform belt. Fascinated, I often had an urge to give them a forceful tug just to see if his butt would fall off.

He knew he was number one on my poop-list for leaving me hanging when I'd gotten stuck in the aforementioned hairy shotgun situation. It happened down in Seminole, the southern part of the county, when I was serving an arrest warrant. The jasper I'd gone after with a warrant confronted me with a double barrel. Remember, the lieutenant had forgotten my call for backup?

By this time, I was back in uniform—by request—and, frankly, winding down my time with the department. I was close to resigning. The lieutenant caught me as I was heading out the door to start the day shift with deputies Bruce Little, Gary Stevenson, Warren King, George McMullen, Ed Kurchinski, and one or two others.

With a big grin (one of those smiles that tells you something's up), he said, "I got a cherry assignment for you and Ed."

He handed over a credit card and the keys to Bailiff Tom Faulkner's new Chevy van that he used to transport prisoners between the jail and numerous courts around the county. He said that Ed and I were to transport five juveniles to the Florida School for Boys in Marianna, better known today as the Dozier Reform School. This was going to take more than eight hours but, it didn't matter, it would be a break from routine patrol. There was no such thing as overtime.

In case of a delay or problem, he said, we were to motel-it in Tallahassee and come on home the next day. No big deal.

ED KURCHINSKI, bar none, was one of the funniest human beings to ever walk on God's Green Earth. A former marine and Palm Harbor barber, he was lean, all wire and muscle and could definitely hold his own in a donnybrook. He told more Polack jokes than the rest of the department put together. His sense of humor was completely outside-the-box. Even when frustrated or pissed he was funny. He saw absurdity in everything he encountered, and rarely stopped laughing. He and I played off each other, giggling like little girls when we were together . . . on or off the job.

The following morning, with a change of civilian clothes stuffed

Deputy Ed Kurchinski

in an overnight bag, we loaded the five kids into the van, that new Chevy van with *PINELLAS COUNTY SHERIFF'S OFFICE* emblazed in big green letters on both sides and rear end. Before we could crank up and pull outta the sally-port a jailer said, "Your lieutenant's on the phone."

"Deputy May," I answered. "What's up, lieutenant?"

Drawling, as if having a second thought, he said as long as we were going to be up around Tallahassee we could drop off a mental patient at the

State Hospital in Chattahoochee. His name was Randall Guy. (Not his real name).

Should we be doing this? "If this guy is a signal 20 (mental case), should we be hauling him in the same vehicle with five juveniles? Is he a sicko, a pervert, a sexual predator? Does the sheriff know?"

"I don't know whether the sheriff knows or not. The contractor that hauls mental patients is unavailable and the captain said to get this guy up there and out of our jail." He paused for emphasis, and then asked, "You wanna call the captain, ask him? Be my guest."

"Nope, but does the sheriff know about this, lieutenant," I asked again. I knew Sheriff Genung was a stickler on all ethical matters.

"Look, this is what the captain wants and you guys can handle it. The van is outfitted to keep those kids and an adult separated so load 'em up and go."

We headed north on US-19. The juveniles and Randall Guy were divided by a steel fence running fore and aft at the center of the van. The driver and passenger seats were separated from the back area by a similar fence that allowed prisoners to be viewed.

So, here I am back in uniform, a 34-year old crime fighter babysitting five incorrigibles and a dingbat. What the hell's happened to my career?

It was a tiresome one-hundred twenty-five mile haul to Chiefland and the kids, full of spit and vinegar, acted-up and annoyed the hell outta Randall. Their behavior was care-free, as if they were heading off to summer camp. Unperturbed and all-knowing, Randall said, "You guys think Dozier's gonna be some kinda picnic, don'tcha? Well, it ain't. I was up there a long time ago and it ain't nice. You all better watch your rosy red butts . . . that's all I got to say 'bout that.'" Born and raised in St. Petersburg, Randall easily discussed his life and events of the day and seemed normal compared to other mentals I'd dealt with in the past. But he had a lot of squirrel in him. He'd cut and run four or five times from the state hospital and always ended up back in St. Petersburg. He had no place else to go.

Chiefland, in those days, was in the middle of nowhere and we stopped to gas up and fill up on burgers and fries. Ed had a problem paying with the county credit card. To save time, he paid the bill out of pocket. Apparently, the folks at McDonalds had never been asked for a receipt so the manager wrote it out on a McCheese Burger bag. We were deep in the boonies and, in those days, credit cards were a rarity. Taking our charges to the john, one at a time, was worrisome and time consuming. Randall, an adult, looked to be in pretty good physical shape, so, I had to keep one eye on the boys and one eye on Randall in case he turned rabbit.

One of the lads moved over close, pushed his fingers through the fence and asked, "You guys do this all the time?"

"Do what?"

"Haul prisoners."

"You're not a prisoner."

"What am I then . . . if I'm not a prisoner? I'm locked up. Can't go nowhere."

"Juvenile court says you're a delinquent. That's why we're taking you and your buddies to Marianna, the boys' school."

He continued, "What's your real job, then?"

"Ed and I are road deputies. My real job is patrolling, working out in the county, driving those green and white cruisers you see all the time, taking complaints and keeping bad guys off the street."

"Have you ever been to Raiford, before?" He was asking about the state prison.

"Yeah. I've hauled prisoners up there a couple times. Why?"

He asked, "You ever see the electric chair?"

"Y'mean old Sparky? Well yeah, I got a tour once and saw it." I laughed, "They asked me if I wanted to sit in it, just try it out. I said thanks but no thanks, didn't want to."

"What's it look like?"

I said, "It's big and it looks heavy . . . made outta oak, I think, and has a lot of leather straps and buckles. It looks pretty intimidating, uncomfortable. Not the kinda chair you'd wanna sit in, kick up your feet and read a book. I had to laugh, though. There's a big sign on the wall behind the chair that says DANGER—HIGH VOLTAGE. You'd think people working there would kinda know that, wouldn't they?"

"My daddy's in Raiford," he said, "been there a long time. Me and mom use to go visit but she divorced him. I ain't seen him in a long time."

He let go of the fence, and turned to watch Ed take the cuffs off Randall and slam the van's back door shut.

Back on the road, we headed for Marianna to drop off the juveniles before it got late. After another 190 miles of tedious gas stops and toilet breaks we reached Florida School for Boys. Before we could get outta the van a middle-aged man hurried from the office, straightening his pants and shirt. His hair was tousled and lipstick spotted his face. He seemed unaware of his appearance. Astonished, Ed and I fought to restrain ourselves and not go into hysterics or fire-off a wisecrack. To Ed, nothing was sacred and I half expected him to nail the guy. Expressionless, Randall gawked, "Son of a bitch! Things ain't changed around here one bit."

With a straight face, the superintendent explained, "Its summertime and, y'know, Wednesdays are lazy days around here (at Dosier)." He said he encouraged his staff to take afternoons off once in a while. Yeah, right! We processed the paperwork and said a quick goodbye to the kids. I left thinking, in a few months they'd probably be back in Pinellas County, on the streets and into more mischief. As we pulled away from the Marianna Campus, Ed slapped the dash, "Five down, one more to go."

RANDALL GUY: The drive to Chattahoochee was less than twenty five miles. Ed snatched up the paperwork, "This shouldn't take long. We'll get ol' Randall checked-in, grab some chow and head for home." But after an unreasonable wait, Ed marched back with a grim look on his kisser. He opened the van door, leaned in wide-eyed and said, "Randall, dammit, you didn't run from Chattahoochee, you're supposed to go back to McClenny, on the other side of the state, over by Jacksonville!"

Randall said, "I know it."

"Well, why in the hell didn't you say so?"

"Nobody asked me."

It would take one hundred and eighty miles of winding back roads to get us to McClenny. So we called Lt. J.T. Unruffled, he said to take Randall to the Leon County jail (Tallahassee) for the night, book a room at the Holiday Inn and, "First thing in the morning take your signal-20 (mental case) on over to McClenny, then come on home." No big deal.

We drove on in to Tallahassee, a name meaning "old town" by the Appalachee Indians. Less sophisticated then, it was a settlement of grits, boiled peanuts, sweet tea, pecan pie, rocking chairs, and thick drawls. At the jail they obligingly placed Randall in a holding cell. Ed asked the sergeant in charge, "Where's the best place to get something to eat and a little something to drink? I need a Seven and Seven . . . maybe three! But we got to be careful 'cause we're driving a marked sheriff's van. Wouldn't do to get busted for DWI, now would it?" There were belly laughs all around.

The sergeant said the Holiday Inn had a decent café, "But the Bullfrog, a couple blocks over from here, is a place you can get the best fried catfish and hushpuppies in Florida. I guarantee. We grease-down over there at lunch time." Then he snickered, "But, you boys ain't gonna get no booze in this town. Leon County's as dry as a popcorn fart." This guy was Rod Steiger straight out of *In The Heat Of The Night.*

"Yer kidding!"

"Nope! That's the way it is, *boys.*" He looked us over, and then his tone shifted, and became confidential. Here we were inside the Leon County jail, and he's looking over his shoulder to make sure no one is listening. That was a little spooky. "But," he whispered, loud enough to be heard across the street, "Let me tell you what you can do. There's a club out east of town—on Old St. Augustine Road. It's really a private juke joint fer just men, see? It's what we call a bottle club and it's owned by a Tallahassee police captain. The deal is, you're supposed to be a member by buying a membership card, y'see, and have your own bottle on the premises. That's why it's called a bottle club, see?" He was talking to us like we had just come ashore at Miami. He rattled on, "What they do is charge you for set-ups, y'see, and snacks, y'see? But in your case—you being johnny law, from outta town, and all—well, just asked for Pete the manager, show him your tin (badges) and tell him I sent'cha."

"In fact," he continued, "I could probably get a road deputy to run you boys out there, but you'd have to find your own way back to town." He was coming across like Slim Pickens, the character actor.

"Thanks a lot, Sergeant, but we'll manage," I said.

Outside, Ed asked, "How much money you got? We can pay for the hotel and eat on the sheriff's credit card. But, I spent most of my cash at McDonald's in Chiefland."

I said, "I got a ten dollar bill and two witness checks. Counting everything, I'm holding all of nineteen bucks and some silver."

We checked into the downtown Holiday Inn and the front desk declined to cash my witness checks or our personal checks. Although I was in uniform, I guess that wasn't enough ID. Not to worry. Where there's a Willie there's a Waylon. After we'd changed into our street clothes, I said, "You know, Ed, I'm damn-straight gonna wear my Stetson tonight. Intuition tells me this town requires a Stetson." Out the lobby door we went in jeans, cowboy boots, London Fog jackets, S&Ws tucked in our belts and Sheriff Don Genung's Stetsons set low on the brow.

||||||||||||||||||||||||||||||||||||||||||||||||||||||||||||||||||||||||

"When you look good, you feel good."
Saturday Night in Oak Grove, Louisiana
—Song by Tony Joe White

||||||||||||||||||||||||||||||||||||||||||||||||||||||||||||||||||||||||

We found the Bullfrog Café and feasted on some of the best fried catfish this side of Mobile Bay. The total tab came to $8.16, not counting tip. Miss Millie Colter, owner, sneaked us a couple chilled Buds, cashed my witness checks and scoffed when I told her the Holiday Inn wouldn't. "Cautious bastards," she said. "But, you know, boys, the town merchants get screwed a lot, especially when the Legislature's in session. Each year, when everybody's here to conjure up laws, this town gets flooded with politicians and shade tree lobbyists. They come in from all over the southeast. It's good for my business, 'cause I deal in cash on the barrelhead." She told us how to find Old St. Augustine Road. Instinct would tell us how to get to where we wanted to go.

Suffice to say, overloaded with poor judgment and misdirected courage, we piloted the sheriff's brand new white Chevy van with *PINELLAS COUNTY SHERIFF'S DEPARTMENT* emblazed on both sides . . . and on the rear! . . . in large green letters to the bottle club called Plato's Retreat. We parked in a stand of trees on the dark, far side of the gravel parking lot, and made our way through a maze of luxury automobiles and pickups loaded down with dog boxes and gun racks. In speak-easy fashion, we flashed our IDs at the bouncer at the door, told him sergeant so-and-so at the jail sent us, and asked for Pete. We were swept in with handshakes and slaps on the back.

Well, to make a long story short (I know it's too late), we partied-hardy, witnessed an old fashion knock-down, drag-out bar brawl, which requiring us to lift our drinks and step outta the way and mind our own business. Booze? We drank our share (and somebody else's) before walking out in the early sunlight to the cooing of mourning doves and . . . because we were designated special guests in Leon County that night . . . no bar tab. We drove back to town, slept a couple hours, had a Holiday Inn breakfast, retrieved Randall Guy and struck out for McClenny, clear-eyed and bushy-tailed (sort of). Randall wanted to bet big money that we had had more fun that night than he did.

At McClenny, everyone welcomed Randall back *home* like the prodigal son. There were hugs all around. We—Randall, Ed, and I—were treated to a nice lunch. When ready to leave, we asked the staff the best route back to Clearwater. After a lot of hemming-and-hawing and butt-scratching by white-uniformed people, Randall stepped up, pointed through the big glass door and said to go five miles that way, then take such-and-such state road west to such-and-such divided highway, head south twenty-some-miles and we'd spot signs directing us to Tampa-St. Petersburg. We shook hands all around and walked out. On the way home Ed joked that Randall would probably make it back to Pinellas County before we did.

Two or three years after we dropped those kids off at Marianna, Governor Claude Kirk visited the institution and found conditions overcrowded and poor. He said, "Somebody should have blown the whistle on this hell-hole long ago."

That was an interesting comment considering parents and former Marianna inmates had been blowing the whistle about the deplorable conditions for decades. The school operated from 1900 until 2011 and for a time was the largest juvenile reform institution in the U.S. In 2011 the place was the subject of a *St. Petersburg Times* investigation. During the inquiry, victims, both black and white, came forward describing abuses, beatings, rapes, torture, and even the murder of kids by the staff.

TAMPA BAY TIMES—Sunday, February 2, 2014—Governor Charlie Crist ordered an investigation by Florida Department of Law Enforcement in 2009, but its report focused on pointing out the limits of a criminal investigation of decades-old action rather than the potential of an aggressive investigation with modern technology. FDLE discounted using ground-penetrating radar, for example, because tree roots could cause false readings.

It finally took a team of determined USF researchers, overcoming state objections, to lead to the revelations. Attorney Pam Bondi has lobbied on behalf of the Dozier families, and she fully grasps the horrors behind the unmarked graves, evoking the discovery of at least one boy, believed to be age 6, who was buried in a handmade coffin with a marble in his pocket—a small poignant testament to the innocence lost when government shuts children out of sight and out of conscience.

I'm haunted by thoughts and memory. Was that child really so bad that he should have been incarcerated in such a far-away state institution? I pictured in my mind's eye, a defenseless little guy alone in the north Florida internment camp, dying with just one single possession: a marble. What transgressions had he committed that caused him to be placed in such horrible circumstances? What evil could be in the heart of a child so young? Who judged him? Did he have a name? Did he know his name, did he know his mama? Where was she when she was needed so desperately? At the end, was his only possession a marble?

Since 2009, when the revelation of the Dozier atrocities was revealed, I wondered about the fate of those five kids Ed and I hauled up there. They didn't seem really bad. They were perhaps incorrigible but not evil.

It's difficult to understand how or why those cruelties at the state-run Dozier School for Boys were not uncovered earlier. Did no one listen to the anguished cries of mothers? University of Florida scientists have only recently discovered the graves of nearly eighty and suspect that there are more. Crude pipe crosses, rusted and cheap, mark ugly secrets. The remains of children discovered in shoddy handmade coffins suggest hushed-up homicides during a century of secrets. Witnesses have recounted of being told there were two separate burial areas, thought to stem from the era of segregation.

CHAPTER NINE

Bruce Little

I GOTTA TELL YOU about Bruce Little. We've known each other since before Adam picked his first fig leaf. I went to work with the Sheriff's Office (S.O.) a couple years before he showed up. Before that, he did a stint in the Air Force (ours), and worked in a St. Pete jewelry store. I liked the guy right off the bat. That's not like me. I rarely commit to a friendship until I have that person figured out. Am I judgmental? I reckon. He and I may not see each other for months, years at a time but we stay in touch on a steady basis. And when we do sit down and go eye-to-eye after long gaps it only takes a couple minutes to catch up, get up to speed. You know that kind of friendship, don'tcha?

He told me he and wife Jeannie named their son after my son Scott *(The Kool-Aid Tattoo kid)*. That's quite a compliment.

Of all the friends I have in this life (so far), Bruce is at the top of the list, a gentleman of sterling mind and character. He was always good for a laugh, could take (and tell) a joke and was the first to come up with a shrewd and *almost* legal solution to any criminal challenge faced when we working together in Vice & Intelligence (I say that admiringly). Bruce left the S.O. before me, went to college, hooked up with the F.B.I., and then retired. After that, he attended ministerial college and became a Methodist preacher. But, I think I have mentioned all that before.

Remarkably, Bruce continues to do background investigations for the F.B.I. (I call it "Feed Bag Information.") So, he's a preacher who carries a badge and totes a gun, reminding me of that old Glenn Ford movie: *Heaven with a Gun.*

When we started working together Bruce was a smoker. He would start out the day in uniform patrol by pulling in at the nearest 7-11 to buy a pack of smokes. I knew his routine, so I'd hold off, out of sight, until he went inside, momentarily leaving his cruiser unlocked. Then I'd wheel up, turn on his gumball red light, flip on his electronic siren—full blast—lock his doors and zip around the block. Luckily, he always had his keys with him. It was my way of teaching a rookie to always lock his vehicle. That's how I learned, sort of. It didn't take Bruce long to figure out who was messing with him and lock up no matter what. I love the guy like a brother.

BRUCE WRITES: Daryl May was a seasoned patrol deputy when I pinned on my star as a rookie. I rode with him some before being turned loose on my own, and we became friends from the jump. I learned a lot from him and we had a good time. It was his philosophy that you could battle the bad guys and still have fun doing it. Later, as our careers progressed, we became partners on the same shift in uniform patrol and later as detectives on the Vice and Intelligence Squad. Daryl was all about putting serious criminals away, beating them to the punch, at their own game. So was I. Years later, when Miami Vice became a hit TV show, I joked that he and I were the original characters even before it was cool. We've been through a lot together, a friendship forged on trust and respect. I love him like a brother.

One thing about my pard, Daryl—he loved jerking the chain of some supervisors, and there was one vice squad lieutenant who was more concerned with style than substance. Daryl made it a point to pester this guy who suspected us of always being up to something that he didn't know about. He reminded me of one of those self-righteous Baptist preachers who always worried that somebody, somewhere, was having too much fun. He regarded May as a *loose cannon,* of sorts, who needed to be kept on a short leash, even though he knew May was damn efficient and professional. He was constantly suspicious that as soon as we quit work for the night (usually around 1 or 2 A.M.) Daryl and I would go dark and get ourselves into mischief that could get him in trouble with the Sheriff.

One night, after work, Lt. Murray (not his real name), caught Daryl in the old Airport Restaurant and Lounge, just a stroll down the hall from the office. There he was—off duty—sitting at the bar, playing his guitar, entertaining a few old pilots, and Bob Connelly, a Secret Service agent, and other cops and bar flies. The lieutenant admonished him for consuming libations and potentially driving under the influence. After he walked out the door we both laughed about how up tight and red faced the man got when he finally "caught" up with any of his mischievous subordinates.

I told Daryl I was going to give him a new name. From then on, I called him "Moon," 'cause he was always making waves—inside and outside the office. Fifty years later, he is still "Moon"—'cause he's still making waves.

I don't know how true this yarn is because I got it second hand (maybe third) but the story goes that during one of those very late after work gatherings at the airport lounge, Moon was sitting at the bar and, as he was want to do, writing his daily activity reports on bar napkins. While sipping his second or third adult beverage for the evening he began studying the model airplane hanging low, just over the cash register on an island behind the bar. Parked on the other side, in direct line with Moon and the airplane, sat Lt. Murray making goo-goo eyes and chitchatting with Jody, the bar-tender/owner of the place.

Now it was no secret that Moon held just a smidgen of animosity towards our good lieutenant because of two petty suspensions he'd received from him when they were both still back in uniform.

So, Moon reached inside his London Fog jacket, removed his trusty snub-nosed S&W, did something with it under the bar, raised the gun in both hands, lined up on the model airplane, and cocked the weapon. Making a child-like airplane noise, which immediately got Murray's attention, he pulled the trigger— SNAP!

Murray flinched and Moon made a whining crash diving sound and then—BOOM—an imaginary airplane crash noise. Detective Warren McNeely, used to May's antics, glanced over and Moon opened his hand to show six shiny hollow points.

There was a lot of clamor, cussing, and commotion—even threats—but Jody, one of those strong, no-nonsense, take-charge personalities, got things quieted down, pointed at Moon, saying something like, don't ever do that in my place, again. Moon was a grinner.

(L-R) Detectives Bruce Little and Daryl May — Florida's Sheriffs Star Magazine

SAVING SOMEBODY'S BACON

But, here's a story I know first-hand. My bud, "Moon" May, still disagrees with me, insisting he didn't save my bacon.

It was a Saturday night, sometime in the summer. I was a one-year patrol deputy working for the Pinellas County Sheriff's Department. I had just enough experience under my belt to feel fairly confident of my ability to handle about any kind of routine call my dispatcher might assign me. And, I enjoyed where I was working that evening. It was the "3 to 11" (evening) shift and it was always busy, especially on Saturday nights. Zone Two was an area of unincorporated county that encircled Largo—a small, mostly blue collar suburb of nearby Clearwater. And the folks I encountered were, generally speaking, decent, hard-working people who, ah yeah, liked to drink and rowdy-up on weekends. But for the most part, these folks respected the uniform of a Deputy and gave little trouble if one of us rolled up on a complaint.

This night was going to be different. My patrol car radio crackled. Then I heard, "Zone Two." It was the voice of Rufus Shirley, my no nonsense dispatcher who, as a retired veteran of the Florida Highway Patrol, had forgotten more about being a cop than I would ever know.

I answered up, "Zone Two—go ahead."

"Zone Two . . . see the bartender at the Corner Bar, there at Clearwater Largo Road and Belleair Road. He's got some kind'a disturbance going on. I don't have a back-up available at the moment. I'll try to get somebody over there as soon as I can." I knew the place and location immediately—a sleazy gin mill just north of the Largo city limits. I was not that far away, less than five minutes. I pulled into the half empty parking lot with the single red "gumball" light on my cruiser announcing my arrival.

What I didn't know was, a few blocks away, Daryl was on a call, taking a missing juvenile report from a father. After hearing radio send me to a bar disturbance, Daryl asks the father if he'd mind riding along to make sure I was going to be okay. In today's world, it's unimaginable, with all the red tape, rules and regulations, having a citizen on board while heading hell-bent-for-leather to a bar fight. But, that was Moon. He could make a decision and multitask.

As I stepped through the door, I didn't need the bartender to tell me the problem. Five goobers, all brothers in their twenties, and a young woman, were raising some kind of hell, drunked-up and acting mean with pool cues in hand.

"I want this bunch outta here," the barkeep called out. "I've told 'em to leave, but they won't go!" I turned to face the group. Having already cowered the customers and bartender, they now figured to mess with the law. They should have known better. Liquored up as they were, they foolishly moved in mass in my direction. The lead drunk whipped out a long, thin pocket blade commonly known in the south as a "grapefruit knife."

Now, in those days, our only contact for help in dicey situations like this was our car radio, portable body radios with mikes attached to officer's shoulders was technology not yet available. So, when something like this went down, we were alone and on our own. I guess that's what made the job so interesting. One had to rely on his own judgement, initiative, and creativity.

As the surly six came after me, I began hurriedly backing out of the bar toward my cruiser. This had gotten hairy. Halfway across the small parking lot, I realized I wasn't going to reach the car before they got to me. Like a pack of frothing mongrels, I'm certain they sensed how vulnerable I was feeling right then. Outnumbered, and threatened with deadly force, I instinctively went for the service revolver I had been issued as a rookie, a Smith & Wesson .38 Combat Masterpiece (stuffed with hollow points)—but which I had never felt the need to draw in self-defense until that moment. With the group of disorderly drunks advancing some ten to twelve feet from me, I drew down, ordering them to stop. At that same moment, almost as if in slow motion, I still vividly recall (now some 50 years later) a second Sheriff's cruiser sliding in close behind me and stopping, and the happy appearance (for me—not them) of my buddy and shift partner, Daryl May, arriving to back me up (which we all tried to do for each other especially on these kinds of calls).

I recall, that in an instant, May leaped from his car, a very large and menacing nightstick representing serious authority in his hand, yelling as he charged at a dead run. Long story short—my cohort hit Randy Redneck blistering hard, spreading him and his blade across the tarmac. The others immediately cowed down, submitted to the inevitable arrest they knew was coming, and with the help of other arriving deputies, the motley crew was hauled off to the county slammer to sober up.

The lot of them was charged with *drunk & disorderly.* But I charged the guy with the knife, with a felony—assault with a deadly weapon with intent. He later pled out and got some hard jail time. They were all a part of the same rowdy family who had a local history as sorry asses.

When the dust settled, I turned to Daryl, whom I would come to work closely with in later years as detectives on the Vice and Intelligence Squad—and who remains my best friend to this very day—saying to him, "Daryl! Man, you got here just in the nick of time! Ya' saved my bacon!" Only to have him reply with the wry humor that would later make him famous and beloved to many . . . "Nah, 'ol buddy—it sure as hell wasn't *your* bacon I saved." He pointed his nightstick at the bleeding heap at our feet and said, "I saved his sorry ass . . . 'cause you were gonna put holes in him."

CHAPTER TEN

"Little Red Riding Hooker"

"You can lead a whore to culture,

But you can't make her think."
—Anonymous

THERE WAS AN AMBULANCE chaser in St. Petersburg that I loved messing with. Larry What's-His-Name was a lawyer and an award winning prick. For a $1,000, he once represented a Tampa tart that got sentenced to 90 days in the county jail for "hustling" . . . we called it the Crowbar Hotel . . . and he got her out in three months. If he was to take Viagra, he'd just get taller. Larry had chased and caught countless flashing red lights, and should have owned his own ambulance service to save on overhead.

Buster Tagg, a local P.I. (Private Investigator), passed the word to Lt. George McNally, that a hooker was working the St. Pete Yacht Club and south county beaches. He had a phone number. McNally assigned the case to me. I guess because I was the best looking detective in vice. I was handsomer, smoother, and more experienced than Bruce Little or Gary Stevenson or Warren McNeely or rookie Frank Holloway.

Man, I'll hear about that. *I'm only kidding guys!*

I called Pansy Gooch (not her real moniker), told her my name was Dudley Tucker. My story was: I was in town overseeing the grand opening of a new Winn Dixie grocery store. I tried chatting her up, but she seemed preoccupied and promptly quoted her fee: kind of a "take it or leave it" brashness. We set up a *rendezvous* for the following afternoon. I wasn't looking forward to the caper.

Detective Frank Holloway came along as backup. I met the little darlin' in the bar at the Holiday Inn on US-19, just north of the overpass, near 42nd Avenue. One hundred dollars was a lot of money back then. With a light roll of fives and tens in my pocket, I parked myself at a corner table. Holloway, with his back to me, sat hunched over a drink, casually surveying the scene via the bar mirror behind the liquor bottles. The three-martini lunch crowd had dissipated, and there was no one else in the place except the bartender—(sounds like an old Sinatra song, doesn't it?).

Overloaded with amateur swag and sass, my "date" blew into the bar like her daddy owned the dog tracks. Adding to all the paint on her pout, she wore life-threatening spikes and a petite skintight red sheath that looked like it had been spray painted on her. It was proper, in those days, to say a female had a nice figure. But this child had a dynamite body and an ass on her like a $40 mule. Toned down she would have been smokin' hot.

Before I could catch my breath, she pocketed her fee, downed a double Bloody Mary and performed a vanishing act on two king-sized shrimp cocktails. She even coerced me into buying her a pack of Camel smokes. She was cheeky, I'll hand her that. With an off-beat sense of humor, she waved her lighted cigarette like film star Betty Davis, took a long deliberate drag, blew a stream of blue haze at the ceiling fan and declared, "Camel Shit Cigarettes; not a fart in a carload."

"Your job sounds boring, Dudley. What do you do to jazz up your life?"

I bit my lower lip, "Well, I could show you pictures of my harmonica collection."

"I don't think so. By the way, how'd you get my phone number?"

"Why didn't you ask me that yesterday?"

She persisted, *"How'd you get my phone number, Dudley?"*

"It was scribbled in a phone booth at the St. Pete Yacht Club," I said dryly. She knew it was BS. "What's the difference, Sweetie?" I reached over and patted her thigh high.

"Well, don't pass it around. I'm choosy." Then mockingly, she said, "Okay, let's get to it, *Sweetie,* time's a'wasting."

My two beers were working on me so I leaned over, said, "I gotta turn me bike around."

"What's that mean?"

"That's Brit-speak for 'I gotta hit the head, go to the john, drain the dragon.'"

"Okay, but scurry. I got lots to do today."

Returning, I stepped to the bar, paid the barkeep, "Keep the change," and made eye contact with Holloway. Before taking the side door exit, and heading for the motel room, she turned to me, looked up into my eyes and casually brushed her hands against my sides. It wasn't a come-on. She was checking for a weapon. I wasn't carrying. I fell in behind Pansy. Beholding her backside was like watching two little critters wrestling in a gunny sack. My daddy would have said she'd make a bulldog break its chain.

She turned and gave me that look, "I don't French kiss, alright?"

"I don't do snuff but I'll try to control myself."

"You got a good job?"

"Yeah, sure. I been a company man for a long time. I don't know nothing but Winn Dixie and I don't wanna know nothing but Winn Dixie!" A decade before, a company supervisor had made that mindless declaration to me.

She said, "I could get to liking you Dudley; you're cute."

"I get to town pretty often. Y'know, I sing and play the guitar, too. Do you like campfires and sing-alongs? Do you know the words to *Kumbaya?*"

Her big browns shot me that look that said *gimme a break.*

Before I could pocket the room key and shut the door, Miss Pansy slapped a Trojan in my paw, and pealed out of her miniscule red sheath. Single-handedly, she popped the snap on her black lace bra and unholstered a powerful set of gazongas. From the belly button up she resembled the bumper on a '55 Buick Roadmaster. Standing tall in spikes, she skillfully wiggled out of her micro-skivvies.

Stepping out of my penny loafers, I sat on the edge of the bed, and leisurely removed my clip-on paisley, and unbuttoned my shirt. The clip-on tie should have been her first clue. Only cops, bouncers, and school bus drivers wear clip-ons. In a scuffle, the first thing an antagonist snatches is whatever's flapping in the breeze. A clip-on tie breaks loose like the handle on a two dollar shovel.

Standing impatient, and *nekked* as a jaybird, she said, "C'mon coach, let's shoot some hoops, it's time for romance."

Moments later, wearing my shiny S&W cuffs in the back seat of a sheriff's marked unit she called me a cheap sonofabitch. I felt slighted. In one sitting, she'd scarfed down enough shrimp to have left-overs at a Cajun wedding. "I knew you were a cop!" she snarled. That hurt. I thought I'd pulled-off the neck-bones and pig-knuckles spiel pretty convincingly.

Daddy owned a trucking company. Mama operated an art gallery. Miss Pansy chose not to forfeit bond, instead she hired Larry the Prick to fight the charge with mama and daddy's dough. There was no way their little flower, the mother of two darlings, could have committed such an indiscretion.

The following week, Larry, sans client, persuaded J.P. Judge Dan Whitney (not his real name) to hear the prelim in his chambers. In the end, as the result of my testimony, Little Red Riding Hooker was bound over for a jury trial.

Sarcasm was his second language and in a lame attempt to be cute, Larry asked, "So, deputy, what have you done with Miss Gooch's unmentionables, tack them to the office bulletin board?"

"No, Counselor, I mailed her lacy undies to your wife in a plain manila envelope." With a reproachful look, Judge Whitney informed me I was out of line. He pointed out that my professionalism was lacking, that he was certain Sheriff Genung would not approve of one of his detectives conducting himself in his court in such an amateurish manner.

Pompous and dull on the bench, Whitney, who, I'd never seen ruffled or at a loss for words, was married with a nice family, was a distinguished associate of the St. Petersburg Yacht Club, presenting himself as a respected member of the community. But he knew a lot of us cops knew better. What he didn't say, spoke volumes. He was not all that fond of the sheriff or me or other vice detectives. This was because, as a member of an elite sports club, he, along with a bail bondsman and another judge, and several other lawyers, had barely escaped prosecution earlier for bringing a lone hooker named Diane Fleetman into Florida on a train for immoral purposes.

So there I stood—a real smartass—in the presence of two lawyers. One smirking. The other dryly lecturing me on my absence of propriety . . . I heard the word *jurisprudence and respect for Florida's court system,* and the reasons why we all must conduct ourselves with decorum and respect—or something to that effect. You get the picture.

Even so, Larry the Prick must have realized the strength of my case against Miss Gooch because, before a trial date could be set, he entered a plea of *nolo contendere* for her. She walked off with a fine and the beginning of a rap sheet.

Outside of busting Larry's gonads, I didn't particularly enjoy making that case, anyhow. It made J. Edger Hoover's boys happy when they came around for their monthly gathering of crime data. Had I gotten the Pansy Gooch complaint first, it would have gone into the shredder. Morality cannot be legislated. Street hookers and call girls and courtesans have operated in Florida since Ponce hit Pensacola. Enforcing those types of laws wastes time and tax money. Only when drugs, organized crime, pimps, or underage kids are involved should the law step in. I found out that higher class hookers are incredibly honest in their own fashion. They have an aversion to out-and-out lying unless it's to keep from going to the slammer.

After the dust settled I wrote a song titled:

"I NEVER MET A HOOKER I DIDN'T LIKE"

Politicians make me shake and CPAs make mistakes,

And anytime you need a cab they're out on strike.

Out of all the folks I've known, there's one group that stands alone,

'Cause I Never Met a Hooker I didn't Like.

Long after, out of idle curiosity, I contacted Deputy Paul Pierce, supervisor of records at the sheriff's office, to check out Pansy Gooch's rap sheet. It turned out to be lengthy, including everything from prostitution to hard drugs to grand theft. The old black and white mug shots were not complimentary. She looked like seven miles of gravel road. Life had not been good to Ms. Gooch.

Let's skip ahead in time. I am no longer a cop but working a gig at the Marti Gras Lounge on Tampa's Dale Mabry Highway. It was a weeknight. Things weren't exactly dead because there were a few patrons scattered around the darkened lounge. Even the Mafia associates, who hung out at the bar, had taken the night off. I'm pretty much doing background music for people having quiet conversations and drinks, intent on making it an early night.

All of a sudden, a well-dressed, middle aged man whooshed in, entangled with an attractive younger woman. He wasn't exactly leading her by the arm . . . even though she was following along with her left hand in his front pocket. He seemed pleased. It was a muddled tango which usually takes place in hotel elevators or between mating flamingos. They bee-lined to a back table. There were lots of whispers, giggles, and canoodling . . . a little touchy-touchy here, a little touchy-touchy there.

A trained observer can spot critical *horniness* a mile away.

Guess what? It was the Right Honorable Daniel Whitney who was now in my chambers, so to speak. To quote Sheriff Andy Taylor, "Well golleee, Barney, don't that just beat all?" With his tie a little wonky, hair slightly mussed, he dropped a room key on the cocktail table and ordered champagne, oblivious to me or anything else outside the range of his table.

I took a long moment to dedicate the song *I'm In the Nude (Mood) for Love* to the "new couple at the back table." With big smiles they answered, "We're just old friends." They raised their glasses in my direction, and drank up but in doing so His Honor got a good look at me in the spotlight and became distracted. He appeared less horny. "Who the hell is that guy up there" was his feeble expression. What was going through his mind is called profiling. Cops do it. Judges do it. You may not be able to come up with a name right away, but you sure pick-up and tune-in to a reliable vibe—it's either good or bad. The vibe he was getting was not all that good. I was delighted.

I put down my guitar, stepped off the stage and made my way to the table, shook his hand and said, "Good to see you Judge. What brings you to this side of the bay?" He still had that puzzled look. "You don't recognize me? Daryl May—I used to be with Pinellas S.O. a few years back." His eyes kinda glazed over as the connection began to sink in. He quickly introduced me to his "cousin," said they had to leave, motioned to the cocktail waitress for the check and nearly knocked me over making an exit. Not quite grasping the moment, the "cousin" followed along—this time—with her hand in her own pocket.

LAUDERDALE: One winter season, I was entertaining at the Sheraton in Lauderdale. The multistoried hotel faced the Atlantic Ocean. It was a high-end property with lots of classy traffic, both vacationers and business clientele.

From the stage I had a clear view through the expansive tinted windows of the hotel's front desk and house phone. Classy, fashionably dressed women would arrive and get on the phone before taking the elevator, which was close by. People at the reception desk apparently understood that kind of traffic was good for business and looked the other way.

During a break, Cortez, the bartender, introduced me to a stunning Hispanic sitting alone next to the waitress's station. She had long jet black hair, dark penetrating eyes and perfect teeth that must have cost her daddy a fortune. She was tastefully made up and looked to be on the other side of thirty.

"Daryl, say hello to Jayla. You two have a lot in common. She's an entertainer, too."

"Hi Jayla. Nice to meet you," says I. I knew what she was. She offered a well-manicured hand and kiddingly said, "Yeah, it's true. I've got a hamster that does weird tricks and I make a lot of money at high schools." She was born in Miami, and her parents had fled Castro's Cuba. She said, "You do some kind of funny stuff. Were you really a cop? Did you ever work vice?"

"I did, I worked in that division for about three and a half years, why?"

She smiled, "Well, let's just say, I'll bet you're a better singer than a vice cop. Right Cortez?" Cortez showed a lot of teeth and nodded.

Eventually, she took a call on the bar phone, gathered her belongings, pinched me on the butt and left. This was a long time before cell phones so Jayla made use of the Sheraton bar phone to conduct business. Later, I sat around while Cortez closed down the bar. He told me Jayla worked the better hotels along the strip. He said she was in the $1,000 a night bracket, that she had a college degree, and could discuss literature and classical music with the best of them. I didn't ask but wondered if Cortez, like cab drivers and bellhops, got kick-backs for his extracurricular services.

TAMPA: There was a bar on West Kennedy, owned or "fronted" by Mafia hitman Johnny "Scarface" Riviera. It had the typical dim interior and backroom for clandestine skullduggery. One night, Bob Prine, the restaurateur, drove me, Det. Leigh McEachern, and a couple of other vice guys to the Riviera Club and introduced us to "the owner." Riviera Club . . . Johnny Riviera? Duh! I was caught off guard and it was definitely unappreciated by Scarface. I don't think anyone shook hands. Prine thought it amusing. We didn't stay long. Cops were fairly certain, but never able to prove, that Mob Boss Santo Trafficante Sr. gave Johnny the task of slitting the throat of his former Florida gambling boss Charlie Wall.

Later, during my early guitar picking days, I worked a club on West Kennedy. The place seemed familiar and I finally realized it was the same bar where McEachern and I had had the face-off with Johnny "Scarface" Riviera.

In any case, the place had now changed hands, gone through renovation and was owned by a woman, whose name I no longer remember. The property had a new name. One night when I showed up for work, she called me over, said confidentially that there would be a 9ish gathering of "ladies" on the dark side of the room. She asked me not to do my show, but until the meeting was over to provide a little background music.

It was okay with me. On a Monday night there wouldn't be that many people coming by anyhow.

On time, the front door opened and in streamed a parade of females: black and tall, white and small, brown, short, skinny, some looked like they'd been on the road too long. Their warrantee had expired. Some were beautiful, looking like Buccaneer cheerleaders or office execs headed home to fix dinner for the family. Others wore the usual outfits we see in mugshots: tight turtle-skirts, or short-shorts and kinky boots. There was enough black leather to make Hugh Hefner sweat.

Holy hustler, Batman! A total of forty-four *ladies of the evening* showed up. I know. I counted. For an hour, I did appropriate love ballads, like *I'm in the Mood for Love,* except I changed the lyrics to *I'm In The Nude For Love.* I sang Willie and Waylon, too. *She's A Big Breasted Woman In Love With A Small Handed Man.*

I don't know what the meeting was about—it was subdued and orderly—but when it ended several attendees came over to compliment me on my choice of music and, I gotta tell you, those ladies flat knew how to tip.

Out of all the folks I've known, there's one group that stands alone *'Cause I Never Met a Hooker I didn't Like.*

CHAPTER ELEVEN

Perri

WHILE I WAS STILL in Vice & Intelligence, my small daughter Perri, maybe about 7–8 years old, and a student at Clearwater's Belcher Elementary, stayed one afternoon after class to help her teacher with a project. It was her sweet nature to always want to help. She was innocent and loving, perceptive and gentle. In those innocuous days my kids, along with the other neighbor kids, walked or rode their bikes the three or four blocks to school.

When I got home that evening, Marilyn told me that something scary had happened to Perri as she walked home alone from school. An older boy on a bicycle had followed her and said he was going to do things to her, things she had no way of understanding. I asked Perri to tell me what happened. She told me precisely what the boy had said and did to her. She said he'd stroked her shoulders and the back of her head. Confused by this stranger, several times her size, she came home wide eyed and frightened.

My antenna went up and I was flooded with anger. Only weeks earlier Bruce Little and I had attended a sex crimes school in Melbourne, Florida. The instructor was Special Agent Walter V. McLaughlin, the legendary FBI Agent who pioneered the whole concept of early identification of sexual predators. He was the definitive national expert on the subject. For me, the week long course was mind-numbing and it took a strong stomach to sit there eight hours a day, looking at grainy black and white photographs of blood, gore, and mayhem and being made aware of the despicable acts of perverts who maimed and murdered.

I asked Perri if she could identify the boy. Precocious and articulate, she said she could. The following afternoon, without informing my lieutenant, I picked her up at Belcher Elementary and we drove the few blocks north to Oak Grove Junior High. I would handle this problem in my own way. It was personal. I took her little hand and we walked around and among the several bike racks. Out of the hundreds of bicycles she pointed at a green one, looked up and said, "That's his bike, Dad, right there." She had spotted it much too quickly. I had my doubts. I said nothing but hoped she could recognize the boy.

We went back to my unmarked sheriff's car. She stood quietly on the floor board, resting her little arms on the car dash. She was alert and unafraid knowing she was safe with me. While waiting for school to let out, we talked about her day and we laughed about other things. I wanted to keep her mind off the problem at hand. Finally, the bell rang and hundreds of students swarmed from the building. Some headed for the sidewalks, while others got on busses or rode off on bikes. Only a few were left behind, including that particular green one. Encouraged, I began thinking my little girl might have made the right call. Waiting a while longer, more kids exited the building and Perri pointed at a tall and lanky youth sauntering alone across the parking lot. She said, "That's the boy, Dad." Sure enough he went to the green bike. Before he could unlock the chain I walked up on him. I was outfitted in a dark suit and tie. I flipped open my ID, told him who I was and asked, "Howya doin'? What's your name?"

He said, "Bobby Lee . . . what's wrong? Whatta you want?"

"Is Lee your last name?"

"No. My last name is Carlson, Bobby Lee Carlson." *(Not a real name.)*

Nonchalantly, I said, "Ah, I just wanted to talk to you for a minute, Bobby Lee." I turned and pointed, "See that little girl over there in the black car?" He nodded. "Well, she said you followed her down Belcher Road yesterday afternoon about this time and said some ugly things to her, told her what you wanted do to her sexually. You touched her and it scared her pretty bad." I drilled him with a stare.

He blinked. "Did you do that Bobby Lee Carlson?" He denied it. He had never seen her before. I friendlied up and asked, "C'mon now Bobby Lee, are you real sure about that?"

He became arrogant, said, "Yeah, I'm sure! She's lyin.'"

Nearly my size, the boy was long haired and pimply faced. I moved in close and shifted gears. "Let me tell you something you scrawny (expletive)." It's easy to abhor an adult pedophile, a pervert. Yet, I had never felt that much anger towards a person so young. I exploded, "That little girl *is my daughter!* She spotted your bike before you got outta class and she fingered you before you got your wheels. If you keep lying to me I'm gonna kick your skinny butt all over this school yard in front of God and all these other kids. Then I'm gonna take you to the county jail. If you want to tinker with sex you can have a shot at it in a jail cell. How does that sound, Skippy?"

Stepping back, he wilted and fessed up. Said he was "sorry, didn't mean no harm," and wouldn't have "done nothing like that to her." I told him to take a long and close look and if he ever so much as got near my kid again, his young life, as he knew it, would be altered. It was a bluff. What mattered was that he believed me. I walked him to the office, and explained to the school principal what had happened. He said he'd follow up with the S.O. juvenile authorities the next day, after I'd written and submitted my report. Satisfied, I went back to the car and told Perri she'd have no more problems with the boy. But I reasoned with her, that she shouldn't walk home alone, that she should always stay with the other neighbor kids and come straight home. She understood.

I asked Perri, "Are you okay now? You're not afraid anymore?" She said she wasn't but she stayed close. I held her and told her I'd never let anything bad ever happen to her. She was my little girl and nothing could harm her, ever. I promised.

I was satisfied with my course of action. Above all else, a man is responsible for the care and safety of his family. I would take whatever measures necessary to get that job done.

Bobby Lee Carlson eventually dropped out of high school. Occasionally, I checked on his whereabouts and his activities. He pulled a stint in the county jail for assaulting a girlfriend. Then one summer night he savagely raped a girl and beat her to death. He left her battered body in the muddy ditch on East Bay Drive just west of the Thunderbird Drive-In, a short distance . . . as the crow flies . . . from our home on Valencia Way. He was convicted of murder.

PART II

"They say, best men are molded out of faults,

And, for the most, become much more the better

For being a little bad." —William Shakespeare,
"Measure for Measure"

George Alden May

1916-2009

MY DAD, GEORGE ALDEN "Al" May was named after a second cousin, a successful real estate developer, who, as a captain in the Indiana Cavalry, participated in the two bloody charges at Pea Ridge, Arkansas, during the Civil War. Adjoining stones in the Potomac, IL cemetery mark their resting sites. As I climb in years I am convinced that—if I have a sense of humor—I got it from Dad. I also believe, without a doubt, he is an ancient soul . . . as is his dad, John "Jack" Erit Charles May (1874-1950). I hope to write something about both men in my next book.

Dad sang in a pleasant baritone voice and played the guitar, harmonica, and fiddle. Not a great musician but good. He was a carpenter that, as a pastime, carved small wooden figures of hound dogs, skinny old women, cowboys and such . . . and painted landscapes in the fashion of artist Grandma Moses. Two of his seascapes hung in the living room and were titled *Breaking Waves* and *Breaking Wind.* He had a quick but dry sense of humor.

Dad was in his late 80s, when he and Mom were down from Illinois visiting Brenda and me at our Clearwater home. One afternoon he was at the dining room table with his back to me tapping lightly on something. I asked, "What are you doin' Dad?" He said his hearing aid batteries had died. I suggested we take a quick drive to the nearest Walgreens. Leaving the drugstore, he was happy to have bought new batteries on sale. On the way home I asked him how long a hearing aid battery lasted. He looked at me out of the corner of his eye and said, "What?"

He was putting me on but I played along and repeated my question, but louder. "How long does a battery last you—Dad?"

He said, "Aw, about two weeks if I don't say 'huh' too many times."

CHAPTER TWELVE

"The Sirens' Call"

"The cave you fear to enter
Holds the treasure you seek."
—Joseph Campbell

I BEGAN DABBLING IN creative writing and poetry when I was in high school. After leaving St. Pete Junior College, and eventually going with the S.O., I got serious about songwriting. Friends, hearing my stuff, invited me to parties. They'd say, "Bring your guitar." I'd show up, break out the Gibson, do a few of my ballads and tell a few funny cop stories. When you make people laugh, they like you and, in turn, that made me feel pretty doggone good. I could go for a couple hours. It was good for the ego, self-esteem, and I realized I was on to something that could be rewarding.

I also recognized the success of Trooper Jim Foster, the good looking sergeant who was a public relations safety officer with the Florida Highway Patrol. I knew Jim through our work in law enforcement and our mutual interest in country music. He hosted a local television show and had a hit novelty song with United Artist Records called *Four on the Floor (And a Fifth Under The Seat)*. Using his position with the F.H.P. as a springboard, he later launched a successful political career and served ten years in the Florida House of Representatives.

Raised on a farm in central Georgia, he moved to Florida after serving in the Air Force during the Korean War. He loved country music and, like me, taught himself to play the guitar as a youngster. Some of his songs were recorded by top country artists.

From then on, Jim recorded regularly for various labels, including Plantation Records owned by Shelby S. Singleton, the Nashville producer behind Jeannie C. Riley's 1968 mega hit *Harper Valley PTA*. In the late 60s and early 70s, Foster hosted a 15-minute Sunday TV show, *"Bring 'Em Back Alive,"* on Tampa Bay's WLCY-TV Channel 10 and voiced traffic safety public service announcements for radio stations throughout the Greater Tampa Bay Area. He left politics in 1982, and retired. He was my friend, a nice guy, and he encouraged me.

CLAY HART: My career switch to entertainer gained momentum after I became friends with Clay Hart, who was doing a single act at Schrafft's Motor Hotel on the hill, just walking distance from downtown Clearwater. The dining room, facing west, had a magnificent view of the harbor. Every evening the sunsets were stunningly different. The intimate lounge, called Harry's New York Bar, had impressive acoustics, soft lighting, thick carpet, and red velvet walls. With gilded mirrors, the place gave you the feeling of stepping into a nineteenth century house of ill repute. Sitting in one of the low cushiony chairs, one could imagine drinking spiked sarsaparilla in a Gotham bordello, and listening to Scott Joplin plinking *Maple Leaf Rag*. It was a convenient place for professionals to meet and impress clients. Bill North, the bartender, was a hustler of eye-catching ladies.

Daryl May (Artwork courtesy of George Miller)

In his 60s, and not exactly handsome, Bill had an overabundance of *something* that was totally foreign to the rest of us in this man's world.

Marilyn and I, with friends, caught Clay's show on my nights off. Sometimes, I'd slide by after finishing the 3-to-11 shift. He was (and still is) a talented dude, about my age, with a million dollar smile. He sang everything from pop to folk to Merle Haggard. His strongest suite included ballads and Broadway show tunes. In my humble opinion, when Lawrence Welk introduced Clay to the nation on his popular TV show as a country singer, he sabotaged all chances of Clay becoming an even bigger star. Clay was too good-looking and too great a singer to be identified as "Country" which consisted of, in part, Webb Pierce's honky-tonk and Bob Wills' western swing and Johnny Cash's country rock. He had the appearance, charm, and polished refinement of an Anglo Julio Iglesias, who was the hot pop artist at the time. Clay could easily have been the Josh Groban of that day and age.

Before I forget, there was a conversation that supposedly took place between Willie Nelson and his wife, while they were in England, relating to Julio Iglesias. Willie, who has performed or recorded with every artist on the charts, heard the Latino heart throb singing on the radio and asked his wife, "Who's that?" She told him it was Julio Iglesias. Willie asked, "Who's that?" She said Iglesias was the hottest singer in the U.S. and Europe, selling millions of records in different languages. Purportedly, Willie said, kiddingly, "He can't be too big; he's never sung with me." Lo and behold, Julio and Willie's recording of "To All the Girls I've Loved Before" would top the charts.

Clay Hart launched his singing career as a strolling troubadour at Dick Siple's Garden Seat Restaurant, another landmark eatery that looked out over Clearwater Harbor. The restaurant was considered the epitome of genteel dining. Clay knew only a few popular ballads and he would start out on one side of the dining room, and by the time he'd crooned his limited repertoire he had made it to the other side of the dining room. By then, there would have been a turn-over in customers, and so he'd go back and start the stroll all over again. He loves telling the story about the biggest tip he ever got at Siple's. A gentleman diner shoved a $20 bill in his face and told him to take his guitar and go back to the other side of the room.

After Clay and I became acquainted, he encouraged me to play his Martin D-28 guitar on slow nights in the lounge. I'd sing my own stuff.

During my time as a vice detective I became a pretty good public speaker. I spoke to the media, presented drug programs at schools and to social and business organizations. I would also go along with Sheriff Genung to state and national conferences, and talk to gatherings about the evils of acid, pills, hard drugs, and that *dreadful* weed, marijuana. I even learned to properly pronounce *tetrahydrocannabinol*—shortened to TLC—which is marijuana, and used today to successfully treat or prevent nausea and vomiting caused by cancer medicines. In my opinion, the stuff should be legalized in Florida. That said, I was not intimidated getting in front of crowds to speak or perform.

After I started showing up at Clay's, deputies and other cops turned up with their wives and friends to catch me playing on Tuesday nights. Someone would invariably call out, "How about doing *Hey There Fuzz?*" If customers didn't ask for it, Clay would. *Hey There Fuzz* was my first original song about cops. I wrote it tongue in cheek, for me, Frank Holloway, and Bruce Little and a few other mates at the Sheriff's Office. It was a corny take-off on uniform deputies. But what the heck, people liked it, it went over well. I was encouraged. At parties, *Hey There Fuzz* was always requested. Fellow cops identified with the hokey lyrics because, at that time, police vehicles were not equipped with air conditioning or seat belts. Florida's summers were made worse by our long sleeved white shirts, green clip-on ties and heavy leather. It was a big deal when the sheriff finally purchased cruisers with AC.

HEY THERE FUZZ

By Daryl May

Ah, he works alone beside the gun

All alone beside that gun

All through the night

In the pale moonlight

Workin' alone beside that gun.

Well, the juke box's loud but can't be heard

The noise is from the 53 [Avenue Tavern]

The bright lights are on

A fight don't last too long

Smell from a stink that's just been stirred.

BRIDGE: *Hey There Fuzz with your bright shinin' star*

Chrome .38 and those air conditioned cars

Good guys and bad guy

Rifles and riots–three K-meetings

And those barroom fights.

A bar–a fight–a broken head

And all for something some drunk said

A busted mouth is free

Black eyes that barely see

And all for something some drunk said.

This new scenario fascinated me. Clay worked an 18-hour week and pulled in $200. Eleven dollars an hour was excellent money in the 60s. I was working a 40 to 50 hour week at the sheriff's office for a lot less. Marilyn, my wife, was employed with the First National Bank, downtown Clearwater. She brought home enough to pay the babysitter, the power bill, and some groceries. By then, we had three kids. But with Clay's encouragement, I became motivated. To be an artist and live on one's own talents no longer seemed like a pipedream.

I watched as Clay performed, watched how he chatted with people in the audience. He did a little patter or narrative between songs, told a couple jokes and always mingled with customers during breaks. Contrary to the routines of most entertainers and bands, who worked a rigid 45 minutes before punctually taking a 15 or 20 minute break, Clay, ever the professional, performed for as long as the audience stayed with him, often two or more hours. He loved entertaining, the singing, interacting with people. When he took a break he'd go to every table to say hello, speaking with everyone in the room, thanking them for coming to see his show. People love to be recognized. By following that friendly demeanor, Clay established a strong fan base. He knew regular customers by their first names and, in turn, they felt he was their friend.

Sometimes, on slow nights, he'd sit with his guitar at customers' tables, or push a couple tables together, and sing and do a little one-on-one.

In the 50s, Genung, Hillsborough Sheriff Ed Blackburn, and a few other influential people came up with the idea of creating the Florida Sheriffs Boys Ranch. Among those organizers was restauranteur Johnny Leverock, who held the first fish fry to raise money for the program at his Pinellas Park restaurant. I volunteered each year to help work traffic on US-19, getting cars and busses in and out of Leverock's large parking lot. Eventually, the event got so big it was moved to the Pinellas County fairgrounds on East Bay Drive in Largo.

On one occasion the sheriff asked Deputy Oscar Underwood and me to line up entertainment for the annual Leverock's fish fry. Oscar was a fine singer and talented mandolin player and persuaded several blue grass professionals to perform free, gratis. Recording artist Lenny Dee—a close friend of the sheriff—gladly gave of his time, talent, and comedy and he was always a big hit. I asked Clay Hart if he'd be a part of the show and he got a bit of a surprise. He'd never worked a crowd that large. "There must have been five hundred people listening to me at one time," he marveled. Of course, his performances with Lawrence Welk on national television would be viewed by millions for seven-plus years.

Clay persuaded Sean Kelly, Schrafft's general manager, to hire me while he was away performing out of state. I took two weeks' vacation and gave it a try. I got $200 a week, loved the job and was convinced I could handle the gig even with my limited experience. Come hell or high water I had to give this urge to perform a shot.

At that time, there was thought to be some kind of regulation that Florida lawmen were prohibited from working in an establishment with a liquor license. Lt. Jerry Coleman confided to me that Sheriff Genung had sent him over to see how I was doing at Schrafft's. The sheriff then asked the state attorney's office to confidentially review the rumored *regulation* with the Florida Attorney General in Tallahassee and it was determined to be inapplicable. Unbeknownst to me, Genung had become an early admirer and would write a personal, touching sentiment for my first album *Laughing On The Inside*. He wrote:

> *"Daryl May was one of Pinellas County's finest Deputy Sheriffs—possessing love, understanding, and compassion for others—and is my friend. His decision to change his profession from law enforcement to music and entertainment was certainly a loss to law enforcement but a tremendous asset to the entertainment world, and we are delighted. 'Whatever the wealth of our treasure trove, the best we shall find is a friend.' Sheriff Don Genung, Pinellas County, Florida."*

HENRY CLAY HART III, born and reared in Providence RI., attended Amherst College in Massachusetts as a major in theater arts. Although his passion was in music, he worked as a salesman in a record shop in New York City after graduation and later as a foreign credit analyst on Wall Street. But those jobs didn't last very long. He moved to Florida to pursue a music career.

A few years later he was working a hotel lounge gig in West Virginia, when he was discovered by Big Band Leader Lawrence Welk, who was at the resort for a luncheon on behalf of the Cancer Crusade. Some of Welk's people caught Clay's act and told the boss about the handsome young singer in the bar downstairs. Sight unseen, Welk invited Clay to sing for the cancer assemblage. Welk was impressed and Clay was invited to appear on Welk's network TV show. In July 1969 Clay and his wife were sent airfare to California. After his televised performance Welk asked Clay on camera if he'd like to become a member of the Champagne Music Makers. How would you answer that question on national television?

Lawrence Welk (b.1903–d.1992) was a musician, accordionist, bandleader, and television impresario, who hosted *The Lawrence Welk Show* from 1951 to 1982 and excelled at accumulating wealth. His style came to be known to millions of radio, television, and live-performance fans (and critics) as "Champagne Music". In 1996, Welk was ranked #43 on TV Guide's 50 Greatest TV Stars of All Time. He was born in Strasburg, North Dakota, and grew up speaking German and English. He quit school in the fourth grade and persuaded his father, a dirt farmer, to buy him a $400 accordion, equivalent to almost $5,000 in 2015 ("Gee Papa, it's a Wurlitzer!"). The rest is history.

Members of Welk's musical group mimic his German accent to a "T" and quote his many misspeaks. He would regularly start rehearsals by saying, "Okay bois (boys) and girls, let's pee (be) on our tose (toes)." During one rehearsal, he stopped the orchestra to tell Neil LaVang that his guitar was too "lout" (loud). With the volume already set on "low," Neil reached down, and turned off his amplifier. Again, Welk stopped the band to say, "Neil, I tolt you, your guitar is juss too lout!" LaVang said, "Lawrence I've turned my amp off." Always right, Welk said, "It's no excuse." He told a horn player that "not only can I not hear you Rocky, but you are playing the wrong notes!" Everyone was required to memorize their lines and song lyrics. The exception, of course, was Welk who worked with cue cards . . . and read them stiffly and poorly. During one show featuring music from the big band era, instead of saying WWII (as in World War Two), he read it as "W.W. Eye, Eye," and plodded on, clueless. He refused to do retakes, which took time and cost money.

For one of the TV shows, Clay asked Welk if he could sing *Okie from Muskogee,* a hit song by Merle Haggard. Welk said to him, "Clay, my boy, no one wants to hear songs about marijuana." But, what's really wacky is that somehow or another Gail Farrell and Dick Dale sang *One Toke Over The Line* on a Welk show in 1971. I'm certain Welk had not a clue. There is a You Tube up and running today of the two singing the duet.

Clay was on the show until 1975, and nominated for a Grammy in 1969 with his first hit record *Spring,* but he lost to Johnny Cash's *A Boy Named Sue.* He released other albums, one of which was *Clay Hart: Most Requested Country Favorites.* Clay married show vocalist Sally Flynn on December 6, 1974, and the two became a husband-and-wife singing act that opened for stars such as Mel Tillis, Red Skelton, and Juliet Prowse. They continue to appear in reruns of the Welk Show on PBS, and have toured the U.S. with fellow Welk stars in concert series.

I signed an open-end contract with Schrafft's, and gave my two week notice at the sheriff's office. Supervisors couldn't believe I was throwing away all those years that I had with the sheriff's office to "go play in a bar." On Christmas Eve (1970) I was gone. And I was to have the Tampa Tribune and the St. Petersburg Times do full page spreads on my new career. From the get-go, I was doing basically what I had been doing at parties. I worked in my original songs, adding narratives and a little chatter. I got busy learning new pop and country songs, and performing those new tunes every night.

RUSS KIMBALL: Well, guess what? Even before I could unpack my guitar, turn on my sound system, sing my first song, and tell my first story at Schrafft's, property manager Sean Kelly had moved on and was replaced by a new guy. Russ Kimball, a Yankee, who got his start in the business washing dishes, had transferred to Clearwater from a Schrafft's Motor Hotel in Western, New York.

Kimball was stuck with me. I was someone he hadn't actually hired. He told Bill, the bartender, that my show/act was dull and dreary, that I lacked professionalism. He could have been right. I was new in the business. After a few short weeks, despite excellent articles in the *St. Pete Times, Evening Independent,* and *Clearwater Sun,* which brought in customers (mostly cops) and revenue, he told Bill to let me go. Actually, Kimball fired me three times. Yeah, threeeee times! No kidding. That's some kind of funny. Bill talked Kimball out of it twice, saying I was doing a decent job, to give me a chance. Nonetheless, the third time stuck and I was out of a job. Although the future looked a little grim, I was young and confident. I kept the faith.

One quiet evening in the lounge (before I got fired) I walked over to say hello to a well-dressed, middle aged couple sitting at a back table. He was friendly, said his name was Henry, and asked several pointed questions about my background and songs I'd written. He said he'd just retired from the music business, and that he was

tight with Billy Sherrill, arranger and record producer for the likes of country artists Barbara Mandrell, George Jones, Tammy Wynette *(D-I-V-O-R-C-E)*, Tanya Tucker, and Charlie Rich *(The Most Beautiful Girl In The World)*, just to name a few. I knew that Sherrill was a giant in Nashville's music industry and the creator of the *countrypolitan sound.*

(L-R) Clay Hart and Sally Flynn-Hart hanging out with Daryl on his houseboat, Gypsy Dude, Clearwater Harbor.

Henry said he was impressed with my stuff, and could get my songs to Sherrill. Did I have a demo? For nine years I'd been bullshitted by experts, and had doubts about Henry. I told him that I'd have to bring a demo tape to work. He said he'd come by the following evening and pick it up. True to his word, Henry showed up, said he'd get back to me as soon as he heard from Sherrill.

A few days later, the gentleman came back and handed me a note penned by Sherrill himself that said, *Henry, good stuff but not great. I'd like to hear more. Billy S.*

Guess what? I dropped the ball. I let Henry down. I didn't follow up. Big mistake! Oh yea, I was preoccupied with other bigger plans, thought to be more important. I was going to go to Nashville and record my own stuff, my own way.

Over the years, I entertained at a lot of conventions and national and international law enforcement conferences at Kimball's Sheraton, a huge hotel complex directly on the Gulf Beach, and he and I often crossed paths. One day, during a chat, he paid me a left-handed compliment when comparing me to another local comedian. He told me I was smart enough to get out of town once in a while in order to broaden my horizons and repertoire. In retrospect, if working Nashville, Myrtle Beach, SC, Caribbean cruise ships, and Australia was what he meant, I suppose he nailed it. It paid off.

February 2016: While tying up the loose ends of this book, Brenda asked me what I'd like to do to celebrate my 80th birthday. I said I wanted to have dinner with family and friends at Kimball's Sheraton Hotel. The restaurant is called Rusty's. I've never had a bad meal there and it's the first place we take out-of-town friends. Rusty's is relatively large, chic, and fashionable—featuring American and Mediterranean gourmet cuisine—and no matter how crowded it gets you can actually have a normal conversation with everyone at your table without shouting.

That's what I wanted to do.

The night was memorable. I must admit, Russ really extended himself. He made sure we had an intimate corner of the restaurant, he set up seating for about 30 people and to help celebrate the occasion, he provided unlimited wine for the party. It doesn't get much better than that. Thanks Russ. After all these years, you've made up for that firing way back when *(big grin)!*

Incidentally, just for the record, getting my walking papers at Schrafft's was one of only two times, in my 20 year career, that I got sacked, canned. I must also add that I only got screwed out of a paycheck once, during those twenty years, and that was by the manager of Ireland's Restaurant in Lexington, Kentucky. Two weeks after I left, the eatery-lounge burnt to the ground. It could have been Jewish Lightening. Who knows? I had a pretty tight alibi. On the evening of the blaze, I was 485.7 miles away working a lounge in Columbus, Georgia. *I have witnesses!*

After Schrafft's, I was looking around to pick up another lounge gig, and working menial jobs for Maxie Quinn, owner of Dyco Paints out on Ulmerton Road. I drove delivery trucks all over Pinellas and Hillsborough Counties, crawled inside and scrubbed humongous paint mixing vats, moved and stacked pallets, and supplies in the warehouse. You name it. Maxie and I went way back. He kept after me to stay with my music. He'd say, "You gotta keep doin' it, man."

Maxie was an inspiration and mentor. After a stint in the Marine Corps, he started several businesses, each time falling on his butt and getting further in debt. One day, I asked him, "Max, what are you doing now?" He said he'd just started a paint manufacturing company. My next question was, "What do you know about manufacturing paint?" He said, "Nothing," but he'd learn. I thought, yeah, sure. Well, after years of hard work, Maxie and his wife Pattie built the company into a multi-million dollar business.

TERRY FURNELL: During a gathering of friends, attorney Terry Furnell was pounding out the *Beer Barrel Polka* on an old upright. A former minister, he could play the harmonica, banjo, and piano and do a tolerable shouting impression of Oral Roberts, the fundamentalist TV minister of the day. I was still out of a singing job, so Terry asked me if I thought Clay could help me with my fledgling career. I had doubts. Working hard to develop his own career, Clay was becoming somewhat established in Los Angeles but I just couldn't imagine how he could help me "out there" at this juncture. I certainly didn't want to relocate to California.

Terry, being Terry, said, "Well, how are you gonna find out if you don't go out to California and have a look around?" He reached in his pocket, pulled out a wad of greens, peeled off some $100 bills and said, "Here, go buy a plane ticket."

So, I flew to Los Angeles, and took a look around Hollywood and met Clay's future wife, Sally Flynn. A real firecracker beauty, I've called her "Sally-Doodle" ever since. She's still a beauty, very bright with great comedic timing and razor-sharp humor. I liked her right away. The three of us buddied around L.A.

The Welk Show performers treated me as though I were one of them. I loved the environment. For whatever reason, the girls on the show called me Tex. Maybe the cowboy boots gave me away. Before the taping of one show, I was sitting alone in a front row seat, before the studio audience was ushered in. Welk spotted me, walked over, called me by name, shook my hand and said, "Hello, it's nice to meet one of Clay's friends. He tells me you fellows have known each other for a long time. Please, make yourself at home and enjoy your visit with us." I was impressed. The guy was a real gentleman and a master schmoozer.

One evening, Clay sent me to the famous *Kit Kat Club* in Hollywood, and said to introduce myself to the chic lady manager as his out-of-town buddy. He stayed home because he had a very early golf date the next morning with Welk. At the *Kit Kat Club* things were going quite nicely for me. I was introduced to several people as "Clay's buddy," and was having a nice time making new friends and imbibing an abundance of cheer. Woops, I ran out of cash. So, I high tailed it back to Clay's apartment, found his wallet as he slept and relieved him of his folding money. I'd cash a check in the morning and pay him back. At sunup, while I was deep in snoozeland, Clay went off to golf with Welk, who was known to be wickedly tightfisted, and preached long and loud to his people the importance of being frugal and fiscally responsible. Embarrassed, Clay was forced to ask Welk for a loan in order to tee-off at the fashionable country club.

I said I was sorry.

On a Saturday, Clay, Sally and I motored up the Pacific Coast to Solvang (Danish for "sunny field"), a quaint little town nestled in the Santa Ynez Valley, about 130 miles from L.A. Founded in 1911, it has been a popular tourist destination with fine restaurants and bars, and lovely little shops. It has quiet tree lined streets, horse drawn wagons, beautiful and authentic windmills, and a village green named after author Hans Christian Andersen.

It was a beautiful sunshiny, cloudless day. We wandered around town, browsed a few shops before deciding to hit one of the pubs on the main drag for something cold. We stepped inside a place loaded to the gunnels with tourists. There were three tanned guys huddled around a piano near the front door, doing a good job playing and singing Glen Campbell and John Denver tunes. I would learn they were off-duty Santa Barbara County deputies. The long, rustic, wooden bar stretched from one end of the room to the other, and was packed three deep. We waited our turn to sit down and order. I asked for the coldest Danish beer they served that had a punch. The bartender set a Faxe Extra Strong in front of me. The bottle was wet and coated with tiny ice chips. As we consumed a few brewskies, the bartender strolled by, stopped, took a long hard look at Clay, and said, "Hey, I know who you are! You're that singer on the Lawrence Welk show." He disappeared, and came back with a guitar and shoved it across the bar to Clay. He stood there with an expected grin that said, play something. Play anything.

Clay looked at me. I looked at Sally. We looked at each other as customers up and down the bar leaned in to look our way. I said let's do *El Paso* in the key of C. Bang, off we went, ripping up the many verses of Marty Robbins' western ballad, loud and rowdy. We were knocking out some pretty neat three part harmony and shouting long and loud yahoos at the appropriate moments. Fifty or sixty people joined in at the right time to *yahoo* and *aaah-haaa*. Gawkers came in off the sidewalk to see what all the laughing and yahooing was about. Too many people were having too much fun. We, and the whole room, followed up with an extended rendition of John Denver's *Country Roads*. And on and on it went.

What was intended to be a couple songs at the bar actually turned into a brief songfest. Clay and Sally signed autographs, and the owner invited us up to his private dining room for a gourmet feast. There were, maybe, 10 or 15 of us at one large round table. Sitting next to the Santa Barbara lawmen, we exchanged cop stories and jokes. The day turned out to be memorable.

CHAPTER THIRTEEN

Comedy: The Big Stick

NO SOONER HAD I gotten home, when a wine peddler vaguely known to me called. For the life of me, I don't remember his name. I wish I could because he was a pleasant, scoutmaster type guy who was always friendly and looked out for others, doing good turns. He did me an enormous favor and I still wish I could thank him. He told me a Quality Inn was opening in Clearwater on US-19, just north of Gulf to Bay. They were looking for a singer, a single act to play in the bar and lounge. This Good Samaritan had told Marty, the property manager, and his regional supervisor from California about me. Marty asked that I come by, bring my guitar.

About my age, Marty was a pleasant, humble kind of fellow. Mr. California, the other guy, had the personality of a stopped up grease trap. I sat at the bar, told them about my background, broke out my Martin D-28 and sang exactly three songs. Marty hired me on the spot. We signed an open ended contract requiring a two weeks' notice to cancel. My audition lasted less than 30 minutes. Marty told me afterwards that his California boss didn't like me. I was just too &%^$*#% sure of myself. Luckily, one of the three songs I sang was Marty's all-time, number one favorite. I don't remember the song but I do remember singing it, first thing, every night for Marty during the months I worked for him.

Incidentally, after I left the Lost Knight Lounge, the place hosted other entertainers including my friends guitarists/singers Jerry Burr, Al March, and Bertie Higgins now famous for the mega hit Key Largo.

You might ask how does someone go about being a lounge singer and then morph into comedy? As far as I know there still isn't a *Comedy for Dummies* available at Barnes & Nobles.

This is how it worked out for me. I took the Quality Inn gig thinking I wanted to be a simple laid back ballad singer. That's all I wanted to do, just be Clearwater's Perry Como-John Denver-Englbert Humperdinck. I had studied voice, and knew the latest popular songs. What I didn't realize was that, contrary to expectations, the motel was constantly chock-a-block with out-of-town Honeywell engineers. Plus the lounge was within crawling distance for car salesmen working dealerships along Gulf-to-Bay. At the five o'clock cocktail hour the place filled up, wall to wall. When I showed up for work at nine there were always a bunch of guys jukin' and jivin', and well on their way to Schnocker City.

So, when you have 35 to 50 sober folks who have shown up to see you entertain, out for the night, paid a babysitter, wanting to be entertained . . . and you have eight or ten leftover rowdies, short circuited on Jim Beam, who really don't give a rip how loud and disruptive they are . . . what the heck do you do? To survive, I began taking them on from the stage via the microphone. I became Clint Eastwood, Rodney Dangerfield, Don Rickles, and Arnold Schwarzenegger all in one entity. When they got loud, I became aggressive.

I'd hit back with lines I had learned as a deputy, like, "You know they gotta be car salesmen because they can entertain themselves for more than two hours with a flyswatter."

"I guess the tractor pull was cancelled tonight." Or, "He sells cars because his degree in puppetry and grit sculpturing has yet to provide meaningful employment."

If Jack Smith mouthed off at me from the bar, I told the audience that, " . . . when Jack was circumcised they threw away the wrong end." If Bill White became disruptive, I'd ask the barmaid over the microphone to give Bill White a drink on me. "Make it to go!" If that didn't shut him up, I'd say give him a double shot of alum.

If Al Black was jabbering, I'd yell, "Hey Albert, where'd you learn to whisper, in a saw mill?" Usually they quieted down, or became embarrassed when I drilled them in front of strangers or their buddies. Sometimes it worked. Sometimes it didn't. My reputation, although deceptive, convinced them I could physically take them on if it came right down to it. It never came to that but I always got my way. I could not, would not be intimidated.

At that time, the Cold War was raging. But, America was standing proud and tall, reaching for the stars and beyond. On the other hand, since Barack Obama, our glorious leader, has occupied the White House, he's scratches a few red lines in the sand and redirected the director of NASA to try to make Muslims 'feel good' and like us. NASA's boss was ordered to *reach out to the Muslim world* as one of the space agency's top priorities. Byron York, columnist for the Washington Examiner, characterized Obama's space policy shift as moving "from moon landings to promoting self-esteem." With ISIS growing stronger every day, you can see where this has gotten us thus far.

America and the USSR were going at each other tooth and nail; playing nuclear *I dare you* games at every turn. This stimulated our massive space and defense efforts. I got to know the Honeywell engineers who sometimes hinted what they were doing for the American cause. Texan Albert Hopkins (not his real name) was one of those guys I suspected of working on secret programs. He came up missing for several weeks and when he reappeared he was in a celebratory mood. With Honeywell colleagues, he was chugging Champaign and doing snakebite shooters at a table off in the corner. I went over to say howdy. Albert poured me a flute full, stood grinning and slapped me on the back. I asked where he'd been. "I've not seen you around for a couple months, Albert. What're you celebrating?"

"Just got back from Cal-eye-forn-eye-A! Been out there working on a project," he said. "On the very first go-around, we successfully shot down a missile with another missile. That's like shooting a bullet with a bullet." I said, "Dang Albert. Should you be telling me this stuff?" He raised a glass, said, "Let me tell you something, Coach! We could give the (expletive) Russians every (expletive) secret we got and in six months we'd still be ahead of those sonsabitches."

Albert was a character, and had a lot of cowboy in him. His cronies said he could stare down a Rio Hondo rattlesnake. With a couple martinis under his belt, he had a tendency to demonstrate Lone Star bluster. However, I once witnessed his meeker side. It was suspected he was snoggin' his young and shapely secretary. She was a looker. They certainly kept their hands busy under the table playing patty-fingers.

Anyhow, Albert forgets to go home one evening after the cocktail hour. He forgot to go home a lot. On this particular night, he was sitting facing the lounge entrance a la Wild Bill Hickok, when Mrs. Hopkins unexpectedly materialized like Tinkerbell. With the swiftness of a tetchy chicken hawk, Albert spotted his wife-mate from across the smoky room before she could adjust to the darkness. Singing an extra slow version of *Help Me Make It Through The Night*, I watched the scene unravel. As if taking sniper fire, Albert skillfully dropped to the carpet and, like a nasty little grass snake, slithered around table and chair legs in great haste. He withdrew via the fire exit, leaving his faithful secretary alone at their candle lit table with two partially filled martini glasses and two cigarettes smoldering in the ashtray.

FIRST JOKE: I remember telling my very first joke on stage. It wasn't exactly an off color joke but was definitely socially unacceptable—politically incorrect by today's standards. It was directed at the guys at the bar and had to do with Pearl Bailey being attacked every December 7th.

I was beginning to understand what it took to hold people's attention. It was becoming easy . . . most of the time. I could maybe hook up a customer at a table with someone at the bar. "Hey Mike, see that tall guy at the bar with the ugly tie? That's Al Black. Damn

Al, that's the first time I ever saw a tie that wouldn't match a white shirt."

"Al's from Montgomery, Alabama. Mike, aren't you from that part of the country, too? Al played football at Montgomery High. Did you know that all football fields in Alabama are required to be artificial turf? It keeps the cheerleaders from grazing after the game."

I began to expand, got the idea—no I stole the "idea"—of pointing out the peculiarities of small towns and police departments from the late, great Dick Gold, one of my mentors. I started out, like Gold, picking on Largo and it became a strong part of my act.

I maintained that the only qualifications to be a Largo cop were you had to be able to grow a mustache and have at least a third grade education . . . and they would waive the third grade education.

When working at the Sheraton in Myrtle Beach, South Carolina, I did the very same Largo routine on Conway, the county seat. People couldn't figure out how I knew so much about their small political center.

What's the last thing a hooker takes off in Conway? Her bowling shoes.

Later, while working a ski resort 125 miles north of Melbourne, Australia, in the magnificent Snowy Mountains, I focused on Merryjig, a village nestled at the foot of Mount Buller.

"Last week they had to cancel the annual parade of virgins in Merryjig. One of the girls was sick in bed and the other girl wouldn't march by herself."

Australians were astonished that I knew so much about their town. Communities around the world share similar characteristics and traits.

G. David Howard continues to have an excellent, razor sharp wit and an ingenious talent for greeting folks that come to his shows.

He keeps their attention and the show running. When a guest walks into his showroom he will stop, greet that person or persons, and ask their name, where they're from, and maybe find out their occupation. When the next person(s) shows up, he follows the same routine, introducing the new party, with all the details, to whoever preceded them regardless of the number in the parties. He does this all night long. Eventually, when the lounge is full (be it 30 people or 300), David has remembered the particulars of each and every person in the room. I've seen him do it over and over again. He's brilliant.

I never asked for a raise at the Quality Inn nor did I get one. But, I still got the best end of the deal. I got paid for an eleven month crash course on how to become a lounge entertainer. When I pulled the plug, and ending my contract, I went off to Nashville to record my first album of original songs.

During one of Nashville's annual D.J. Conventions, I was staying with friends Frank and Jeanie Oakley at their charming home overlooking the Cumberland River. Frank, a laid back, well-liked music executive, worked with many Nashville artists including Marty Robbins, Jim Reeves, and Faron Young. They also owned a picture framing shop out on Gallatin Road and it kept Jeanie busy just framing pictures for Johnny Cash's House of Cash. Eventually, on a handshake, Frank formed a partnership with Willie Nelson. They put up a sign out front calling the place *The Willie Nelson & Family Country Store*. The business has thrived and is now located across the street from Nashville's Opryland Hotel, and called the *Willie Nelson & Friends General Store & Museum*.

With Frank's help and guidance I got to know my way around Nashville. I was becoming established, connected, finding steady work around the country, and making exceptionally good money. I would soon have a hit song *(Gator Bar)* on the charts by country artist Mel Tillis.

At one convention Frank and I hooked up with my old buddy Clay and his friend Hank Williams Jr. This was before Hank fell off the mountain. Then we ran into Shel Silverstein, who penned *A Boy Named Sue,* the blockbuster hit for Johnny Cash. Shel, a small balding fellow, was a bearded genius who wore old black engineering boots. He could have been the bigger brother of the seven dwarves, and laughed when I, a stranger, asked if he'd just come back from panning silver in the Sierra Madres. A poet, a songwriter, a Playboy cartoonist, a screenwriter and an author, Shel had a bizarre slant on life and wrote two popular children's books: *Falling Up* and *Where the Sidewalk Ends.* He was an amusing character and immediately accepted Frank and me as friends.

We hit it off when we learned we were both from Illinois. He grew up in Chicago, got kicked out of the University of Illinois and knew of Potomac, my little hometown about 30 miles from the college. Tagging along like a beagle pup was Lawrence Welk Jr., a borderline pain in the neck. He was more like an annoying neighbor kid. Junior's celebrity hinged entirely on the fame and wealth of his daddy, Lawrence Sr.

By chance, we ran into guitarist Jimmy Colvard, a primo studio musician, who was one of my studio pickers when I recorded at Scotty Moore's Studio 8. Scotty was Elvis Presley's original guitarist. Colvard was also peddling songs around Nashville written by Jerry Burr and me.

Off hand, Colvard mentioned he was working a private party that evening at the Sheraton. Playboy's Hugh Hefner was throwing a small shindig to celebrate the release of girlfriend Barbi Benton's saucy little tune called *Brass Buckles (On Her Shoes).* Did we want to come along? "Well, yeah!"

I got a bit of a thrill seeing my name printed on the Playboy guest roster right there alongside Lynn Anderson, Don Gibson, Charlie Pride, Jerry Reed, Tanya Tucker, Jeanie C. Riley, Sammie Smith—all Nashville recording heavies. We pinned on our badges, crowded in the elevator and zoomed to the top floor. Bunnies greeted us, saying we should not misplace or lose our badges because security would enthusiastically boot us out. "After all, Mr. Hefner wants this party to be just for his friends." We joined a hundred or so of Nashville's notables nibbling hors d'oeuvre and sipping cocktails offered freely by even more Bunnies clad in web stockings and high heels and little fuzzy cotton ball tails placed you know where.

Hefner's entourage arrived quietly via a back entrance and sat at two ten-top tables facing the stage. The rest of us gathered around, standing behind the host and his party. Colvard and the band did a few numbers before Ms. Benton strolled on stage to perform *Brass Buckles*. She was a talented cutie and sang her heart out. After the show Hefner, pipe in hand, remained seated, gabbing with intimates and whoever approached to say hello. Ms. Benton, nonetheless, mingled as though she were one of the guests. Shel introduced us, saying some nice things about me that he'd only just heard from Frank. She had an impish grin. I was star struck.

After spending 20 years entertaining and traveling the world, with nothing towards retirement in my pocket, I reluctantly took another job with Pinellas County government.

I was working a regular 8-to-5 county job when Clay called me. He and Sally and their band—made up of top Nashville pickers—were booked to work the Florida condo circuit, up and down the Gulf Coast. They wanted me to open their shows. Flattered but apprehensive, I was pretty rusty and didn't think I could get back on stage. I'd lost my edge, my timing, which is essential for comedy. Besides, I was now working one of those "regular day jobs" and doubted I could make it to places as far away as Venice or Ocala for evening shows. Clay said, "Tell ya what . . . the pay's not all that great anyhow. So, come on with us . . . if you feel like doing 15 minutes or an hour that'll be fine . . . doesn't matter. We just want you to be with us. It'll be fun. It'll be like old times. You and me." It was an offer I couldn't refuse.

The first gig was somewhere here in Clearwater. The audience numbered two or three hundred and I certainly wasn't on my game. Clay and Sally saved the evening by doing a knock-out performance. I wasn't surprised. At the end of the show, I was feeling pretty crappy. God bless Clay. He flashed "that" smile (the one with all the teeth), slapped me on the back and said something like, "You'll get your chops back, Roy Gene. Are we gonna do a great tour or what?" Roy Gene is a nickname we still have for each other. It took maybe another show to pump up my confidence and we wowed thousands up and down the West Coast of Florida, from Naples to Sarasota to Ocala.

There was a gag Sally picked up from Red Skelton while touring with him a couple seasons. Backstage she would listen to my act and pick out the one good joke or story that went over best with the audience. After coming on stage and singing a couple numbers she would begin to tell that same joke, the same one that had gone over so well for me in my set. The audience would stare, wonder what the heck was going on. She would stop and say, "WHAT? Don't tell me that Daryl is doing my material. That bum's stealing my jokes!" It would take folks a couple seconds to realize they'd been had. It was a free and easy gig and we had a blast doing those shows.

I've always regretted that the three of us didn't do some songs together, maybe *El Paso, All the Girls I've Loved Before, On the Road Again,* or *Country Roads,* y'know?

After 20 years, I ended my career in show "bidness." Those last two years (in the late 80s), working summers at the Myrtle Beach Sheraton, I was selling my comedy tapes for $10 a pop, and pulling down $900 a week. Hotel manager Glenda Chestnut, my convivial boss, and other staff members treated me like family. We were family. Management continued to throw in a suite with a million dollar Atlantic Ocean view, food, and booze. Tell that to the next bar owner who says he can get guitar pickers for a dime a dozen.

CHAPTER FOURTEEN

SeaWake

SEAWAKE INN, AT THE south end of Clearwater Beach, was my all-time favorite lounge to perform during the winter season. I was there, off and on (mostly on), for thirteen years. The hotel, no longer owned by the Seatons, still stands overlooking Clearwater Pass and Sand Key. Next door, between the SeaWake Inn and the Pass Bridge, is now an unsightly weed and gravel expanse where Stan Musial's Hilton was once located, a dismal reminder of the 2008 financial crash. The SeaWake looks nothing like it did in the 70s and 80s when I was there. In reality, there are very few beach properties that look as they did in the "old days." There are exceptions, of course.

The Palm Pavilion, owned by the Hamilton family (since 1964), has stood beachside since 1926. With a grand view of magnificent sunsets, the place remains a popular eatery-watering hole for locals and tourists. But, the mom-and-pop motels and businesses are mostly gone. The Islander Restaurant (Phillies manager Dallas Green's old hangout), and Henry Henriquez's Pelican Restaurant, a favorite haunt of established locals, are long gone. Mandalay Avenue and Gulfview Boulevard have become featureless strips of high rises, expensive restaurants, touristy surfboard and flip-flop shops similar to Miami and Lauderdale and Key West. But, you can still purchase a shoddy sea shells picture frame or a bright orange plastic alligator somewhere along the thoroughfare. There are few lounge entertainers to speak of anymore accept for my friend and all-time guitar great Sal Beloise who continues packing venues up and down Mandalay Avenue with his singing and witty patter.

Former SeaWake owner Don Seaton was a considerate boss and an astute businessman. Toward the end of our association, we did quite well, revenue-wise, in the Schooner Lounge and besides paying me a substantial weekly salary he volunteered to give me a generous monthly bonus to boot.

Don's parents, Dick and Lenora Seaton, did the day-to-day hands-on running of the SeaWake. They worked hard, were on the job six days a week from sunup to sundown. More often than not they'd work late and take dinner at *Lenora's*, the motel's dining room named after Mrs. Seaton, and have a few toddies and dine. Mr. Seaton had a bit of a temper and after getting into the sauce he would sometimes lose it over some trivial thing that had been building up inside him all day. He'd blow. When ticked off he was a cross between Mr. Dithers, Dagwood Bumstead's old boss, and Donald Duck. I liked the old guy but, at his age, I thought he and Mrs. Seaton worked too hard. He would often tell me, "I'd like to bulldoze this (expletive) bar and restaurant right into Clearwater Pass."

After working the property for a few years, Dick and I eventually had a difference of opinion, you might say. I can't even remember now what it was about. But I assumed my time working in the Schooner's Lounge was over. A few weeks later my contract ran out and I went off to work other venues: the Hilton next door, and Bob Jones' two Clearwater Holiday Inns, and the swanky Strickland's Townhouse Restaurant in Jacksonville.

Don Seaton called. He wanted me to come by and see him at his Travelodge, a few doors from the SeaWake Inn. I was surprised. He asked, "Isn't it about time you came back to work for me?"

I said, "I love working for you, Don. Your lounge is a beautiful little showroom, it's my all-time favorite. But your dad's not gonna let me come back on the property."

Don, always the gentleman, quietly said, "I own controlling interest in the SeaWake. If I want you back . . . and you wanna come back, you'll work there."

Playing a little mind-poker, I said, "Okay, Don, I'll come back but on one condition."

"What's that?"

I didn't think he'd go for it but I pressed on, "I'll come back . . . but your dad can't come in the lounge after 8:30 on the nights I'm working."

He said, "Put it in the contract." I was surprised. Stunned, actually.

Happily, I returned to the SeaWake. Mr. Seaton, always cordial and respectful, stayed on his side of the lounge threshold. The Seaton family: Dick and Lenore, Don and Nan and their kids Daryl, Wendy and Leni—kids I watched grow up—were all great and easy to be associated with during all those years.

For a while the Seatons had a maintenance worker who was handy with tools but illiterate. Even so, from time to time, he was given the task of changing the hotel's lighted sign out on busy Gulfview Blvd. Regardless of how carefully noted his instructions were, I'd come to work and see my name misspelled *"Dyral Mey,"* or *"Don't Furgit Sunday iss Motter's Dey."* Fans thought it was a creative idea for marketing my lounge act. Dick Seaton would often be seen out there with a long pole and box of letters doing a manual "spell check."

I met my wife Brenda in the Schooner Lounge. She was a young mother who, after losing her husband in a car accident, had moved with Rob, her infant son, to Florida from Butler, PA. A part time model, she worked full time as assistant manager at Baldwin's, a fashionable clothing boutique in downtown Clearwater. John Baldwin, a St. Petersburg highbrow, often remarked that taste was "an innate quality acquired by few but which many attempt to flaunt."

Brenda, at that stage in her life, didn't particularly enjoy lounge comedians or nightlife and, for six weeks, resisted her Uncle Vern's persistence to catch one of my shows. Finally, she caved—just to get him to hush—and came in with him on a busy Saturday night. The only table available happened to be up front near the stage. I zeroed in on this tall dark haired beauty wearing a colorful designer dress. I looked at her long and hard, then, with a drink in hand, pointed, saying her dress looked like she'd shot an awning. She says she fell in love with me at first sight. I think she is being kind . . . but, it certainly worked out in my favor.

"HELLO, CALLING PERU."

JOE DONAHEY: One dawdling SeaWake evening, around 10:30 P.M., I was working a small crowd when the phone rang behind the bar. Seldom did George Miller, the front desk supervisor, put a call through while I was on stage. If there was a message for the lounge, George would quietly walk in with a hand written message.

Tim, the bartender, answered the phone on the second ring, looked in my direction, motioning with one hand that the call was for me. As a rule, I would not leave the stage to take a call. Tim insisted. I responded, "Tim, please get a number and I'll call them back."

He said, "It's Donahey." Meaning, it was Joe Donahey, the prominent defense attorney, at the other end. He and I went back to my days as a deputy and he a prosecutor for Claire Davis, the Pinellas-Pasco State Attorney.

Crap, I mumbled, this has to be important or he wouldn't insist. The first thing that crossed my mind was that something had happened to one of my three teenage kids. Over the mic I asked that everyone give me a quick moment while I took the call.

The conversation went like this:

"May?"

"Yeah Joe, everything alright?"

"It's my birthday! I'm having a party at my house and I want you here."

"Well, happy birthday Councilor. I'm working at the moment . . . as you might have guessed . . . and there are paying guests sitting here and, believe it or not, I'm kind'a busy entertaining them."

"I don't care," came back his response. "Bring those people with you. I want you to come to my birthday party. Bring your guitar."

"I'll work on it, Joe." To placate my friend, I ended the conversation, "It's a little slow tonight. Maybe I can work out something, and slide by later."

Back on stage, I apologized, "Sorry about that folks. That was a friend. It's his birthday. He's had a few Danny Boys and wants me to come to his party." I laughed and added, "He said I should bring all of you with me. Wouldn't that be a blast if we showed up at his house at this hour? Actually, he lives over on the mainland. Not far from here." Hmmm.

The more I considered it, the more I thought it was a brilliant notion. This could be a lot of fun! I'd show his skinny Irish butt. I'd just knock on his front door with a gathering of strangers and sing a loud and blustery happy birthday to him . . . and the neighborhood, then drink up his pricey booze. At my insistence, Tim gave last call. Some people paid up and left while some of the braver, more venturous patrons, steeled by booze, caravanned to the birthday party. We were greeted at the door by Donahey, his pretty wife Tena, and their distinguished guests.

As I tell this story, keep in mind that the Honorable George Joseph Donahey, Esquire, ended his celebrated and illustrious law career as a judge with Florida's Sixth Judicial Circuit, initially appointed to the bench by Florida Governor and He Coon, "Walkin' Lawton" Chiles.

When Joe was a pint-sized, grade-schooler running around Bellefonte, Pennsylvania, hustling odd jobs for nickels and dimes, he fantasized of one day playing football for Penn State. Unfortunately, that aspiration was quashed when his parents divorced and he moved to Largo with his mother. For a long time life was not easy for him and his siblings, or his mother who worked long, hard hours as a waitress. If he felt slighted because of his size or hand-me-downs, his approach and attitude to any given task was kick-ass, balls-to-the-wall no matter the job or opponent. After a stint in Army Intelligence near Langley, Virginia, and classes at Stetson Law School and thousands of hours in the courtroom, he turned that Bantam rooster brashness into a formula for success.

In his professional prime, before becoming a circuit judge, Joe and Terry Allen Furnell, his long and lanky, ingenious, off-the-wall partner, made names for themselves across the southeastern U.S. for their high profile, successful defense work.

As a surprise birthday gift, Tena had given Joe his old Boy Scout bugle reconditioned and polished. It was beautiful, and looked as new and shiny as the day Teddy Roosevelt used it on San Juan Hill. Just kidding. Around 2 A.M., Joe insisted that everyone join him in the backyard to hear his renditions of *reveille, assembly, mess-call, tattoo, call-to-quarters, taps* and the Kentucky Derby's *call-to-post.* Because he and I were big John Wayne fans, his version of a U.S. cavalry charge was my all-time favorite. Wanting to please, Joe repeated it more than a few times, improving and improvising with each rendering. Dang, I could see the Duke, bigger than life, up there on the silver screen, a gleaming cavalry saber flashing above his head, leading a charging squadron of mounted soldiers down a grassy hillside towards the camp of renegade Geronimo, or was it Cochise or Mangas Coloradas? It didn't matter. I was into it. I think Mr. John Daniel's helped. I'm sure the neighbors, tucked soundly away in their beds, were into it, too.

Suddenly, it occurred to Donahey that he had a friend in Lima, Peru that needed to know it was his birthday. He decided I would play and sing *Butter Beans* over the phone to his chum in South America. Placing a long distance call in those days needed the assistance of a real live telephone operator. So, Joe and I retired to the privacy of his master bedroom. After some muddled and misunderstood exchanges with the long distance operator, the phone finally rang at the other end. A man, sounding wide awake, was greeted by Joe with, "This is Donahey in Clearwater, I want'cha to hear this. Listen up!" He pointed at me, gave the down beat and BANG, I launched into a long and raucous version of *Butter Beans*. All verses. Some verses twice.

JUST A BOWL OF BUTTER BEANS

Sung to the tune of the gospel song Just A Closer Walk With Thee

(chorus) Just a bowl of butter beans

Pass the cornbread, if you please

I don't want no turnip greens

All I want is a bowl of butter beans.

(Verse 1.) See that girl sittin' over there?

Yeah, the one with the curlers in her hair

She's not in the family way though it seems

She got that way from eatin' butter beans.

(Sing chorus)

(Verse 2.) I got a girl named Josephine

She ate some rottin' butter beans

She don't use no Listerine

So the boys, they pushed her over Halloween.

(Finish with chorus)

At the finale there was much laughter and disjointed conversation. Then Joe grew sober, discovering that he was not communicating with his friend in far off Lima, Peru. The person on the other end of the line was, in fact, a stranger in Lima, Ohio. Realizing the screw up, my lawyer friend launched in to a heart-felt apology but was interrupted to learn the stranger was a long distance truck driver suffering from terminal cancer. He had only a short time to live. He insisted that absolutely no apologies were necessary. Because of relentless pain he was unable to sleep nights and said this was the most enjoyable phone call he'd gotten since becoming ill.

He thanked us profusely and asked that we have a drink or two in his stead.

In turn, we wished him well and a very somber God's Speed.

The evening's festivities ended in quiet contemplation.

Do I miss the business? Yes, I guess I do from time to time. But, I don't have the driving desire—it's not that strong—that I once had. Sometimes, when I catch the shows of Sally Hart or Jim Stafford or Billy Dean or Sal Beloise, I get the urge. But, it quickly passes. I miss an audience, the unrestrained laughter and uncontrolled interaction. Each night, once the audience had been won over, it was a hell of a lot of fun blasting through a show. I do miss the singing, as well. Singing was my connection to my soul.

About halfway through one slow evening, I had turned from humor to sing a slow, soulful rendition of *The Love Theme From the Godfather*. As I finished, the applause was warm and the mood of the room grew a little somber. A well-dressed lad, sequestered in a dark corner with a young and awesomely developed blond, approached the stage. In a heavy but understandable Italian accent, he handed me a ten dollar bill and said just loud enough for people to hear, "Everee time you singa that songa I geeve you ten dollars—oh-kay?" I thanked him and said, "Sure" Stepping back, he tapped the side of his nose with his trigger finger, signaling that we had an agreement, a contract. He was a pleasant enough fellow, having a nice time and, I suspected, he held strong anticipation for later that night.

I don't know, maybe five minutes later, someone at the bar said, "Hey Daryl . . . how about singing *The Love Theme From the Godfather?*" Obligingly, I sang it again with as much feeling as before. The young fellow laid another bill on me, smiled and said, "Yoo signa that songa weeth much feelings. Thank yoo." Before the night was over—with help from the audience—I must have pocketed $60 or $70. My benefactor was happy. I only wish the routine had started earlier. I did pick-up the fellow's drink tab at last call. I hope he scored. I put forth a lot of effort on his behalf.

CHAPTER FIFTEEN

"On The Prowl with Caroline Kennedy"

"A lie will travel halfway around the World before truth can get its boots on."
—Winston Churchill

"WAS IT REALLY CAROLINE KENNEDY WHO ORDERED DRINKS ALL AROUND?" ... was the headline on the front page of the *Clearwater Sun* in July 1979.

TED EMERSON OWNED THE *Teddy Bear Lounge,* a popular nightclub on South Bayway Blvd., Clearwater Beach. He'd brought his family to Clearwater in the 1960s after making it large in the car business in, I think, Chicago. Every night he perched amicably at the big circular bar next to the cash register, and while keeping a close eye on his money, he greeted friends and strangers alike, sipped cocktails with his buddies, smoked expensive cigars, and held court in general. He was a Polack of prodigious proportions, and fancied he resembled entertainer Dean Martin, the king of cool. He had Martin's likenesses stenciled in the glass of the bar's front door.

A five piece band kept his place cranked from 9 pm well into the early morning hours with 60s and 70s standards and rock-n-roll hits. The *Teddy Bear Lounge* was where Clearwater's monied movers and shakers hung out, partied-hardy, and spent money freely.

Upstairs, in the *La Corsair,* Ted ran one of Clearwater's classiest restaurants. Gentlemen were required to wear coats and ties. One could, despite this, get away with a turtleneck or slip in unobtrusively just by being a buddy of Ted's. Bobby Singleton manned the grand piano in the small upstairs bar, fashionably trimmed in polished brass and tiny white Christmas lights. Bobby seldom took breaks and dispensed Broadway and classical music at the drop of a five dollar tip. He made good money catering to upper crust clientele. Bobby, who favored pop legend Barry Manilow, liked guys. Women loved Bobby. Ted loved having women clustered nightly around the piano bar which, in turn, attracted guys and thus business was good.

Jody was the *La Corsair's* single cocktail waitress. She was bright, just out of college, a classic beauty (I'll bet she still is, even after all these years) with a mischievous grin and crack sense of humor. She made great tips just by being efficient and customer friendly.

The *Sea Wake Inn,* my steady place of work, was located a block or so away on South Gulfview Blvd., overlooking Clearwater Pass and next door to baseball great Stan Musial's *Hilton.* It was convenient for me and other beach entertainers, after knocking off work, to slip over to Ted's and help him close out the night.

Though I was Jody's senior by a wide margin we read the same books, had mutual friends, enjoyed kidding one another, and shared beach gossip.

One evening after ending her gig upstairs we bumped into each other in the downstairs bar. She was chilling out, enjoying an after work toddy. I was at the bar with Ted when Jody walked up from behind, put her hands over my eyes and whispered, "Hi little boy . . . would you like a piece of candy?"

I grinned a devilish grin and whispered back, "My mamma told me to never ever take candy from strangers . . . unless they offered me a ride!"

She suggested we go out one evening to dinner. I thought it was a fine idea. It always stokes a guy's ego (or it did mine) having a young beauty make the first move.

A few evenings later we were engaged in trivial chit-chat over an Australian merlot and dinner at Roland & Pierre's in St. Petersburg when she said, "There is a Willie Nelson quality in your singing voice but, I think, you're better. It's obvious you've had training."

Surprised, I asked, "Oh, and how would you know that?"

"Music was my minor at Ohio State." She said, "Look at me, do I look like a thespian to you?"

Jody was easy to look at. "A what?" I asked.

"A thespian!" she said. "You know, one of those painted narcissists that prance around in stage lights, dancing and singing tunes from South Pacific."

I asked, "Really? And what part did you play in South Pacific?"

"Well, it wasn't Bloody Mary."

I said, "Ya know, people do tell me I sound like Willie. Back before I even had ideas of becoming an entertainer I studied voice for a couple years."

"Interesting," she said. "Well, here's one for ya . . . for as long as I can remember I've been told I look like Caroline Kennedy, President Kennedy's kid. Last night I was serving drinks to a table of Massachusetts seniors and they just couldn't get over it, kept saying how much I looked like her."

I could see the resemblance. But, Jody was prettier.

Heading back to Clearwater via Bay Pines Boulevard, I asked, "You in the mood for a little slumming?"

"Sure, what have you got in mind?"

I said, "There's a neighborhood beer and wine joint on Seminole Boulevard called The Evergreen. It's a hangout for the old farts-and-darts mob and off-duty deputies. After finishing the swing shift some of the guys I used to work with end up there. When the place closes they sometimes go out back by Seminole Lake and build a fire. It's their way of chilling out after spending eight hours fightin' crime. They sit around on logs and buckets, half in the bag, packin' heavy armament, and talking trash. We could check it out. If they've got a fire going, we'll drink their beer and listen to the bullshit for a while."

Just for kicks, I was thinking, we'd stop and see what was happening. But, I had a devious motive, as well. I didn't tell her but I wanted those macho dudes to see that their former working partner was still sharp enough to date a young chick. My intent was to sort of milk the situation. I was in that kind of mood.

She thought it would be fun.

It was late Sunday night, but no fire out back, yet. So, we entered the smoke filled joint and felt our way to the bar. As we sat chatting over my beer and her Pepsi, Jody looked around, asked me what game the old guys across the room were playing. I said there was a spike on the wall and the trick was to see how many tries it took to swing a brass ring on a string and hook it on the nail. It was a simple contest that gave the trailer park commandoes a chance to spit, cuss and mingle, match skills, and wager draft beers.

Jody insisted on giving it a try. Sliding off the bar stool, she cheerfully approached the five old timers who were delighted to have her in their midst. After a short tutorial and one or two tries she planted her high heels, cocked her shapely bum, drew the string tight, placed the ring close to her nose and launched it towards the hook on the wall. Bingo, she got a ringer! Jody shouted at the bartender, "I DID IT! I wanna buy drinks for the house." That sounds a bit exaggerated until you realize this was a long time ago when a draft beer put you out forty cents. Anyhow, as Jody played on, Charlie Keim, the owner, moseyed over, "Hmm, that child certainly is healthy. Who is she May, your daughter?"

"C'mon Charlie, cut me some slack, will ya, I'm not that old."

"Well, you're a hell of lot older than her! Who is she… she looks familiar."

Knowing Charlie was sometimes a little slow on the uptake and, me, feeling ornery, I looked him straight in the eye and said, "Charlie, if I tell you who she is will you promise not to tell anyone, absolutely no one? It's just between you and me, okay?"

He nodded impatiently.

Lowering my voice, I said, "Charlie, pleeease don't tell anyone I'm dating Caroline Kennedy." I pointed, "That's actually JFK's daughter."

Charlie looked back at me, "Aw, cut the crap, willya!" Then he turned, stared, got a good long look and said, "I'll be a (expletive) . . . it is! What's she doing in here? What the hell is she doing with you . . . of all people?"

As Jody settled back on the bar stool next to me, I faked a heartfelt appeal, "Help me out here, Charlie, do not tell anyone!" I took a deep breath for emphasis and introduced the two of them. "Jody this is Charlie Keim. He owns this place. Charlie this is my friend Jody." I gave him a long hard wink . . . one that curled one side of my mouth, stressing that he and I shared a really, really big secret.

After he wandered off I filled Jody in on the prank. She put her head down on the bar and cackled loudly. I told her, "Charlie has a one-dimensional sense of humor and delights being on top of all the Seminole trailer parks' tittle-tattle."

We were thoroughly enjoying the moment when I glanced around and spotted Charlie circulating. Clientele began staring our way. He was telling customers there was a big—whatchamacallit—celebrity in the house. I tossed some bills on the bar and said, "C'mon, let's get outta here ....."

Giggling, as we went out the door, she said, "I gotta tell my mom about this."

The next day, around mid-morning, I was sitting with my feet up on the afterdeck railing of my houseboat *Gypsy Dude*, drinking my first cup. The sun was up but not yet July hot. I watched the passing boat traffic and got "howdys" from marina neighbors headed out for a day on the water.

The phone rang. It was my brother Gary, a detective at the sheriff's office. He told me some reporter wanted to talk to me, but he couldn't reach me because I had an unlisted phone number. He said, "The guy's with the *Clearwater Sun* . . . he wants to know about you being with Caroline Kennedy at The Evergreen last night. I wouldn't give him your number, told him, you could be reached at the SeaWake."

"Aw crap! It's a gag that's gotten outta control, brother. Last night I was with Jody, the cocktail waitress from the *La Corsair.* Coming back from St. Petersburg we stopped off at The Evergreen. I thought we might run into a deputy or two. She won a ring-toss with some old guys and bought the house a round of drinks. Charlie was all over me wanting to know who she was . . . and just to screw with his head I told him it was Caroline Kennedy. She favors Kennedy and I thought I was putting one over on just Charlie."

I asked, "What did you tell the reporter?"

"I told him I didn't know anything about it. But, the Secret Service guys were great to work with."

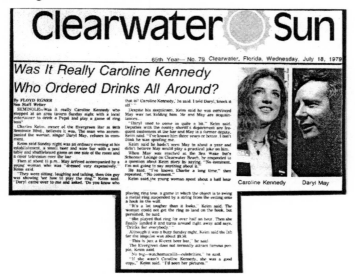

PART III

"You can't soar with eagles,

If you're pickin' shit with the chickens."

The late Margaret Schnur, "Mother -in-Law"

CHAPTER SIXTEEN

Hat Tricks

I'VE WORN A LOT of hats in my time. When I was growing up in Illinois, men wore all shapes and styles of hats. Hats were important. You'd no sooner leave the house without a hat than go to church without a tie. Dad always wore a hat for work and for dress, a classic snap brim when visiting friends or out to dinner. A hat said who you were. I wanted to be like Dad so I wore a regular baseball cap. He was just 20 when I was born. In a way, we sort of grew up together. Strangers thought we were brothers. During the Second World War, it was his generation that put life, limb, and principle on the line in Europe and the Pacific to defend the free nations of the world. I have vivid memories of that dreadful war; fearful recollections as a kid that we might be forced to learn Japanese. I wore a hat then because I wanted to be like those men, those ordinary but great Americans who were dying by the thousands for the tenets and sovereignty of and for this great country. Young people today have no grasp of that notion.

Summer work earned greenbacks for school clothes and books and pocket change, and all the cherry Cokes or twenty five cent banana splits I felt entitled to at Clark Morris's Drug Store. Swinging a flat bladed hoe in July heat made a hat essential. I walked mile after mile in Illinois's rich black earth, chopping renegade beans out of corn fields . . . or corn out of beans. By lunch the hoe had become heavy as an anvil. Although I was skillful at sharpening the long handled tool it did little to make the afternoon slog easier. The Almanac said corn needed to be knee high by the fourth of July. Regardless, there was no shade from the burning sun out there on the rolling prairie. A ten hour day yielded five dollars. On the other hand Dad, a carpenter, made maybe $20 a day. That wasn't bad either.

Before corn pickin' season, bus-loads of kids ventured out to detassel acres of hybrid stalks. It paid pennies an hour. In some cases a hat was utilitarian, part of the "going outdoors" routine. Weighing in at 155 pounds, I'd also put on a straw hat and leather gloves to 'buck' summer bales of hay. It was a dirty, back breaking business but at the end of the day it yielded self-reliance. It made a body feel good and decent. I was earning my way. I and school mates bucked bails, jerked untold numbers of seventy-pound hay bales off the ground and pitched them onto a high tractor trailer or truck bed. It was satisfying to have those fivers tucked in my jeans. I'd earned 'em. No one could tell me what to do with my money or how to spend it. Earning money for the first time gave me a new feeling, a good feeling.

A hat kept the sun off my head and out of my eyes or the snow off my neck. Winter weekends and after school I shoveled grain under gray, dim afternoon skies when daylight was rationed and winter temperatures sunk to freezing and the wind knocked the snot off your upper lip.

My introduction to hard labor happened between the World War Two and the Korean *conflict,* an undeclared war that President Harry S. Truman and the U.N. called a police action. Life continued to be difficult for some people in my hometown. Yet, no one complained about how tough it was or how better life could be. The mind set of my parents and others of their generation was a whole lot different from the old men who bunched up like hunched over buzzards roosting on downtown benches. Those old farts would sit, spit, and whittle and tell anyone, with the patience to listen, just how much better things were "now" compared to how tough it was back in their days when a generation of thousands sailed to France "back in 17 to fight the Kaiser." They'd follow up with the same hogwash stories about when they were young, what it was like to walk miles to school in ass deep snow; *uphill both ways!* Realities didn't get in the way of telling a good story.

In my law enforcement days, deputies dressed out in a grey Stetson straw and a white "good guy" felts in winter. The lid set square on my head and low down on my forehead. It signaled I was cocked, physically fit, and ready to fire to take on all comers or whatever else the job threw at me.

TRICITY DINER: In the 1960s, when country music was actually country and not the flashy and chanting "crossover" crap we hear today, Joyland was a popular Nashville venue. Located north of Pinellas Park on US-19, the place featured local bands and occasional Grand Ol' Opry has-beens. A few miles up the highway was the TriCity Diner where, after last call for alcohol, the all-night eatery filled up with drunken shit kickers and waitresses hustling bacon and eggs and grits to the mob. The place often took on the appearance of a Chinese fire drill.

Around 3 A.M. one Sunday morning, I waited for the Joyland crowd to dissipate before going in for coffee. As I walked in a waitress who knew me pointed towards a darkened corner stool knowing I wanted to avoid the few left-over inebriates. I took the end seat at the counter, placed my Stetson on the stool next to me to prevent uninvited company. A uniform, as a rule, draws attention even in the dark. This night Elvis was pumping out *Viva Las Vegas* on the juke box. Through the din of indiscriminate babble I overheard a female, a few booths behind me; say she was going to go talk to that deputy. "He looks lonely sitting over there in the dark all by his own self. He needs somebody to talk to. That's fer sure." That lonely deputy, of course, was me. The boyfriend strongly advised against it, and I thought her visit had been averted. He must have been her boyfriend. They showed up together and there was tobacco juice on both sides of the truck.

Unexpectedly the woman dropped in beside me like a first string linebacker. In doing so she picked up my snowy white Stetson and shoved it across the counter coated with crumbs, ketchup, and a muddy puddle of coffee. I suspected she manhandled bags of grain at the Largo feed store. She was dressed for a tractor pull. She was ugly, too, which aggravated matters. She smiled demurely flaunting the few yellow teeth left in her head.

"Hi sweetie. What's yer name?"

"Daryl May"

"What's your last name?"

"I just told you. May."

"Don't yooo jest love Elvis?" Her kerosene breath would have peeled aluminum siding. The little darlin' was tanked and over-the-line repulsive. No. I take that back. She was so ugly she'd make a glass eye water. I wanted to tell her what my daddy used to say, that it ain't no sin to be ugly, but you can stay off the streets so people don't have to look at ya.

Dad had a dry sense of humor. I still remember going through adolescence fearing the dark like, I suppose, most kids did. But Dad assured me, if anyone slipped in and snatched me from my bed, that the abductors would surely turn me loose the minute they got me under a street light. Only now is that funny.

Being tolerant doesn't always make it easy reasoning with a drunk, but I forced myself to explain to this uninvited Buckeye Trailer Park chippy that it was my desire to have a quiet cup of coffee, to be left alone, and that it would be in everyone's interest—especially hers—if she simply rejoined her friend post haste. Secretly I was beginning to think she'd be a splendid candidate for the county slammer.

Rejected and offended she stalked away in a huff. "I don't like that (expletive). He could piss off the pope!" was her grievance to anyone listening.

The boyfriend snickered, "Well," he drawled, "I toldja not to go over there and bother him, dumb ass!" And that's how it started. With the temperament of a feed store pinup she bit her lower lip, scrunching up her face like a wad of handy wrap and threw a round-house. He saw it coming, ducked and deflected. The guy in the next booth took the ricocheted but still solid pop on the left ear pan. He vaulted from his seat, knocked an open coffee carafe across the floor. Attempting to prevent a tussle, I accidentally knocked my already stained Stetson onto the floor.

At the height of the melee, eight or ten men and women were yelling, shoving and sliding around on the slop-covered floor. The scuffle quickly became a mob scene. My hat was punted around on the floor like a greased hockey puck. Eventually I managed to quell the fracas without calling for back-up. Pointing, I strongly suggested everyone sit the #%&@ down and shut up ... "or else." I retrieved my battered hat and left by a side door, hoping no one had called the Largo cops. Embarrassed, I lacked the courage to write an incident report or ask the sheriff for a new hat. For $35 I replaced it and kept my mouth shut. I also kept away from TriCity on those nights when it got real drunk out.

STEPIN FETCHIT was the stage name of Lincoln Perry (b.1902). He achieved superstar status on the big screen in the 1930s (becoming a millionaire to boot), and he remains one of the most controversial film actors in American history. His degrading characterization as a lazy, slow-witted, jive-talkin' black man insulted his race in the 1930s and, in my estimation, continues to offend today. A literate and intelligent man, Mr. Perry wrote for the African-American newspaper, *The Chicago Defender,* and evolved an on-screen character called *The Laziest Man in the World.* He was the illiterate subservient that rolled his big eyes, dressed shabbily and wore a sullied baseball cap backwards or with the bill hanging precariously over one ear. It astonishes me that present-day black and white rappers continue to emulate Stepin Fetchit's odious appearance. I suppose it matters little as long as these cartoon characters festoon themselves with solid gold trinkets and chains and gaudy jewelry.

Then there's that guy we see everywhere that's a product of pop-culture. He's the middle aged white guy with a protruding gut and yellow teeth. Hooters girls think he's repulsive but they still cater to his vanity and give him a big smile and call him by his first name.

Sometimes he gets a hug. He's Mr. Big Tipper. He's loud, wears Fukashima wraparounds, cheap flip flops (needing retreads), and a grungy sports jersey. He's still making payments on an old four door Ford F-150 with the Magnum wheel rims that set him back $2,500. You guessed it. He wears his baseball cap with the bill snugged down on the back of his neck. He's a wannabe, but he'll never make it.

I've gotten that off my chest. Let's move on.

Today I wear a United States Army cap ("Est. 1775") square on my head and low on my forehead, like a man. Not with the bill hanging down my neck, coaxing the world to "look at me, I'm cool, and I'm different, I'm cute."

MY SON SCOTT (*The Kool-Aid Tattoo* kid) gave me that official looking U.S. Army cap before leaving on a one year tour to Iraq. Just out of high school, he joined the Air Force intending to make the military a career. His specialty was aircraft electrical systems. In South Dakota he worked on B-52s and Lancer B-1B bombers. In England he worked on the TR-1 (U-2), a high altitude spy plane at the Alconbury Royal Air Force Base near Cambridgeshire. Then Bill Clinton came along and implemented severe cuts in military spending. You remember Slick Willie? During the LBJ years he attended college in England (on a Rhodes scholarship) to avoid the draft. In London he openly demonstrated against the United States' involvement in the Viet Nam war. What a guy. A real winner!

With ten years under his belt, Scott was given the choice of voluntarily leaving the Air Force with a bonus; or if the Pentagon cut back on his job classification, he would get nothing; not even a "thank you" pat on the butt. So he took the piddling bonus, came home, and went to work for the Pinellas County Sheriff's Office, my old alma mater.

He has two stepchildren. Pretty Jessica, no bigger than a minute, became the poster child for the Marine Corps for a while. There was a Marine web site picture of Miss Jessica in full combat uniform during one of her two tours in Iraq. She later became a DI (drill instructor) at Camp Lejeune, North Carolina.

Stepson Derik joined the Army Airborne, made numerous jumps at Fort Benning before going off to combat in the second Iraq War. His primary bitch was that "they" wouldn't let the troops fight the fight.

Because of Jessica and Derik's commitments, son Scott, then in his 40s, felt an obligation to follow their example. He joined the army reserve, the only military service that would take him at his age. He went off and saw the ugly side of war in and around Baghdad. He again took a leave of absence from the sheriff's office to do a one year stint in Afghanistan.

OCALA SHERATON: But I digress. There was a time, back in the 70s and 80s, when if you wore a cap or hat, someone, out-of-the-blue, might say, "I'll give you 50–cents for that hat." To demonstrate you were a good sport, you'd hand it over. It was the Code of the West, sort of.

Late one evening, as I worked on stage at the Ocala Sheraton, a tanned, All-American looking fellow walked in with an incredibly pretty date. He was wearing a plain white baseball cap. I was adept at reading my audience and, that night, the room was with me. Ocala is the heart of horse and cowboy country, so my usual remarks and routine went thusly:

ME: "Hey, c'mon in, big guy. Howya doin'?"

HIM: "Doin' great. Thanks."

ME: "Nice lookin' lady, man. I bet your feelin' a little cocky tonight (ornery grin).

"Hey, I really like that hat!"

HIM: "Thanks, again."

ME: "I wish I had two hats like that. I'd shit in one and cover it up with the other."

He began to grin.

Before the couple got seated, I said to him, pleasantly, over the microphone, "I'll give you 50–cents for that brand new lid." Being a good sport . . . and knowing the drill—he walked to the edge of my stage and handed me his hat. I gave him a dollar and told him to keep the change. The audience snickered.

I swear this happened next. I'm not making it up. No sooner had I placed the newly acquired hat on my bean than a tall blow-hard, dressed in white cowboy boots, cuffed jeans and a turquoise string tie, came roaring through the door. The fellow was on the cutting edge of Ocala chic. Following, in lock step, were five hangers-on.

I asked, "Where'd you boys park your horses?" Alfa-Male laughed, spotted my hat, slapped the bar and hollered, "I gotta have that hat, Sport. I'll give you $5 for it, right now." I lied, told him my daddy gave me the hat on his death bed. I went on to bullshit Bubba Blowhard, telling him I loved my hat. I would never . . . I could never ever part with it. "Never!"

He persisted. Finally, I said, "Tell you what Bubba; I'll sell you my hat for $25 . . . but, on one condition." I waved randomly at the fellow who had just sold it me minutes before and said, "I'll sell you my hat, but you gotta pick up that handsome couple's tab for the night." He said, "You got a deal, Sport!" The caper went down. The audience went wild with table banging laughter. Bubba was pleased with himself. He thought he had stolen the show, impressed his friends and the audience. He had no clue the joke was on him.

To finish the guy off, I pressed the issue, "You know what, Big Guy, you look real gooood in my hat! Why don't you buy a round of drinks for the house?" By then, Mr. Alligator Mouth knew he had overloaded his hummingbird butt. It was too late. To save face, he bought the house a round. All in all, the night cost Bubba a pretty penny.

A TWO-HUNDRED DOLLAR DENIM HAT: As a lounge entertainer I disliked working with props. My good friend Rod Griffith sometimes used articles like rubber chickens, hokey mustaches, or goofy hats to emphasize his show band comedy. It worked for him.

Nevertheless, one day I chanced upon a $14 flat crowned Levi cowboy hat. It was dusty-blue denim, looked great and the price was right. Chuck Floyd, a guitar pickin' buddy, handed me a silver band that gave the lid a nice touch. I wore it when doing my Johnny Cash/Waylon Jennings routine.

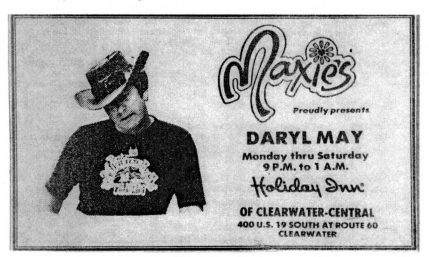

I was working a full house one Friday night at Bob Jones's Clearwater Holiday Inn Central at US-19 and Gulf to Bay. At around 10:30 P.M. I was cooking, the crowd was having a good time, and I was in the zone. Just as I pulled on my new $14 dusty-blue denim and starting singing *On The Road Again*, a Largo High Roller, came through the door with four or five off-duty Largo cops in tow. Although not all that bad looking, he was a guy that couldn't get laid in a whorehouse with a fist full of fifty dollar bills. You know the kind. And so, to compensate, he picked up bar tabs for hangers-on. It was good for his ego.

Leaning on the bar, with a drink in hand, a thumb stuck in his belt, and surrounded by his companions, he interrupted the room by loudly declaring, "When I leave here tonight, ol' buddy, I'm leaving with that hat!" Slightly annoyed, I stopped, pointed and mockingly told him, "Well, ol' buddy, you might leave with my brand new denim hat but you're gonna have to pay for it." He barked, "How much?" Without thinking, I said, "Two-hundred dollars—*CASH.*"

He said, "Bring 'er over here." I set down my Gibson, stepped off the stage, walked through the crowd, and handed him my hat. He reached in his pocket, extracted a wad of greens and pealed-off two crisp $100 bills.

My contract said I worked until 1 or 1:30 A.M. if the crowd stayed with me. But without so much as a shit-howdy, I stepped back on stage, got on the mic and gave last call. I turned off the stage lights and started packing my guitar. Bernie the bartender yelled out, "Hey! What's goin' on? It's too early for last call!" With my guitar case in hand, and headed out the door, I paused and yelled back, "Bernie, anyone with two hundred dollars in their pocket shouldn't be hanging out in a dump like this!" Daryl had left the building. I was gone for the night.

BOB JONES: I mentioned owner Bob Jones earlier. He was a major stockholder in a chain of Holiday Inns and was tolerant of entertainers' idiosyncrasies as long as they made him money. He was a little mischievous himself and pulled an unexpected prank on me as payback for my denim hat walk-out. It happened months later when he hired me again to entertain on Sunday nights at one of his fancier Clearwater Beach showrooms.

Bob had me doing one-nighters in a lounge that featured Hal Harvey & The Affair, a trendy show group with a strong following. He wanted me to work Hal's night off. At first I hesitated, thinking it would be tough to fill in for a six-piece band that did shows and dance sets. I was a single act, played guitar, sang and did comedy. I–did–not–do–dance–sets. Jones enticed me (with cash). I caved. Surprisingly, the gig started off quite well. The place seated over a hundred, and each Sunday night I managed to keep it full with tourists and locals.

So on this one Sunday night, at about 10 P.M., while working a full house, I noticed the cocktail waitresses going from table to table, whispering to customers. Just as I began my Johnny Cash / Merle

Haggard routine, every person in the room stood up and walked out, including the hostess, bartenders, and cocktail waitresses. As the last person vanished, the house lights went out, and the lock on the double doors clicked. I sat there in total darkness with only my breathing audible over the sound system. It was so quiet you could hear a fish fart.

After what seemed an eternity, the lights came back on, and Jones, who was supposed to be out of town, opened the door and stepped in. With guffaws all around, he led all one-hundred plus customers back to their tables. With an incredible show of generosity, he bought champagne for the house and gave me a thumbs-up. Bob Jones had a remarkable sense of humor. It was a pleasure working for him all those years.

YELLOWSTONE NATIONAL PARK: In 2010, Brenda and I were visiting Yellowstone National Park. For lunch we went to the Old Faithful Lodge within walking distance of the famously predictable geyser. The luncheonette was jammed and we sat at the counter for some time waiting while others who had come in behind us were being served. The waiters and waitresses were college kids. Some were busting their buns, hustling food, while one or two stood mindlessly with their thumbs up their backside. An older kid, tall and authoritative, kept strolling by our counter with his hands tucked behind his back like a British pensioner. Finally, I said, "Hey big guy, how long do you think it'll be before someone takes our order?" Surprised, he pulled out his order pad, then looked at my hat and asked, "Sir, what did you do in the military?"

I was wearing the beautiful black and gold U.S. Army hat son Scott gave me before going to Afghanistan. Scott, a veteran Pinellas deputy, is also a U. S. Army reservist. As mentioned, he'd spent a year in Iraq. Many who see my hat will ask what my job was in the Army and I always take the time to explain how I came by the hat. Everyone will say, "Please tell your son we appreciate his service to this country."

This time, however, I was slightly annoyed with this young goober. So, I put on my best military face (which was actually my old deputy's stare), and answered, "Well son, do you know anything about the U.S. going to Iraq and kicked Saddam Hussain's ass?" Wide eyed, he nodded. I said, "Well, as a two-star, I was the guy that worked with the CIA and coordinated all the U-2 flights before and during that bloody incursion. That's all I can say about it, boy." He shot out his paw, gave me a hard handshake, thanked me for my service and scurried off to get our lunch.

Brenda, my lovely bride, leaned over and whispered, "*YOU* are gonna go to hell."

I grinned that shy grin of obedience and said, "Darlin', I just made that young man's day."

Incidentally, that afternoon, Brenda and I were idling along a narrow Yellowstone blacktop enjoying the drive and scenery. Cresting a slight hill, we came upon vehicles parked chaotically in the road. Leaning out car windows, parents and kids were watching a sizable grizzly mamma with three adorable little cubs a few yards away in a clearing of high grass. Nose down and digging for roots and grubs, mamma ignored the gathering audience but the babies, poking their fuzzy little heads above the grass, stared back as if mesmerized by humans they'd probably never seen before.

All at once a large bus skidded to a stop behind us and a noisy mob of Japanese bailed out and scampered around the parked cars to the road's edge, just a stone's toss to nearest wide eyed cub. Armed with all sorts of cameras they pointed and jabbered, capturing the moment. A few minutes later, mamma bear raised her enormous head and snorted and the little ones moseyed along behind her into the nearby timber. With no park ranger present, I breathed a sigh of relief knowing what the animal might have done had she thought her babies were in jeopardy.

Over breakfast, the following morning, I mentioned the incident to a passing ranger. She said it was remarkable how foreigners, despite verbal and posted warnings, seemed clueless about the dangers of park wildlife, and that at least one or two major incidents between man and animal, involving serious injuries, took place each year.

Before walking away, she smiled, touched my sleeve, and said that Yellowstone grizzlies think Orientals taste like chicken.

Lately, I've worn a dark blue military baseball cap with crossed sabers stitched in gold. Every so often, some salty old timer will yell and throw a salute, thinking I was in the U.S. Cavalry. I suppose because of my age (80) and mustache they think of me an officer. It happens often. Each time I smile and reply, "The Second (Cavalry)." If pressed, I will dutifully explain that I actually wear my cavalry hat because after completing a 25-year study of Lt. Col. Charles Augustus May (1817-1864), United States Second Dragoons, possibly an ancestor, my 200–plus page manuscript has been placed in the Smithsonian Museum of Military History—their request—and the West Point Military Library and the prestigious Huntington Museum at San Marino, CA. The work is titled *The Last Dragoon, The Incredible Life & Career of Col. Charles A. May.*

See my website: **www.darylmaycomedy.com.**

CHAPTER SEVENTEEN

Sacred Moment

THERE IS ABSOLUTELY NOTHING more shattering or heartbreaking than losing a child. It defies life's common order. It should not be that way, should it?

My kids grew up. Daughters Perri and Wendy got married. Son Scott joined the Air Force and was stationed in Texas, South Dakota, and England. I left the sheriff's office. Marilyn and I divorced. It was an amicable break. Not long afterwards, Marilyn was diagnosed with breast cancer and fought the horrid disease for nine long and arduous years. It was heart breaking for the kids and me to helplessly see her waste away and die.

Just out of high school, Perri was diagnosed with Hodgkin's lymphoma, cancer of the lymph nodes. She was diagnosed early and after lengthy chemo treatments the disease went into remission. We thought she had dodged the bullet. She married, but doctors told her she'd be unable to have children. Too much chemo. She persevered, said the decision was God's not those in the medical profession and after miscarriages she had three healthy, beautiful kids. Perri was strong in character and flawless and unpretentious as a mother.

The cancer returned. But, worst of all, there was absolutely nothing that I, as her dad, could do. I was utterly helpless as her life slowly ebbed away. On that terrible, terrible day, Perri's husband Jim called from the Pasco County Hospice. Brenda and I had just left Perri after being at her side for several hours. He said, "Perri's asking for you and Brenda. Daryl, you need to get up here as soon as possible."

The dreadful hour had come.

Perri lay quiet as her family and loved ones gathered around. Kissing her forehead and stroking her arm, I whispered how much I loved her. With eyes closed, she smiled faintly and lightly squeezed my hand. Also in the room, besides her children were cousins and aunts, people from Perri and Jim's church. A church lady asked Perri if she were feeling just a little less pain. She said, simply, "No." Then she softly said, "I'm passing." After a slight pause she smiled peacefully and said, "I'd rather not." Then it was over. She was gone.

Grief washed through me like heat lightening. It was an all-consuming pain. I can't remember, as an adult, ever crying. Yet, on this sorrowful day I hurried outside, into the sunlight and sobbed like a child.

I know I was blessed to have her for a daughter and to be there at her side, to be there for her, to tell her how much I loved her and to know that she knew. But there was absolutely nothing I could do for my daughter, my kid, still my little girl. I was eaten up with helplessness. I had grieved the loss of my parents. Their passing was not the same. They had both lived long and, I think, meaningful lives, almost reaching 94. But, losing Perri was different, a lot different. I was thankful my parents weren't still around. They would have taken Perri's death real hard. It's been six years now, I'm waiting for the loss and sadness to lighten. But, I know it will always be with me. With the passing of years, I miss her even more.

The finality of Perri's sickness hit me between the eyes months earlier when she arrived late for a Mother's Day picnic at Philippi Park with Jim and the kids. It would be her last. She came up the hill using dual walking sticks, saw me watching and smiled, assuring me it was just temporary until the chemo was finished. I knew better. She had never lied to me. But, this was a fib. I knew it was and allowed it. I could stand a lie easier than I could stand the truth. It alleviated a measure of emotional pain for her . . . and me. She was thinking of me, her daddy. She deserved better. But, life is not fair. There are no guarantees, only inventories.

The day of Perri's memorial, I was a lucky guy to have Brenda at my side. She was like a mother to Perri. My daughter Wendy, who has my sense of humor, laughingly refers to Brenda as, "My wicked stepmother." Besides Wendy, I was also comforted to have son Scott and his family as well as my brother Gary, from Illinois.

My old friend Bruce Little, who had just lost his dear and beautiful wife Jeannie two weeks earlier, drove down alone from Jackson, Tennessee to be with me. Sandy Sharpe, my fighter pilot buddy, drove from his home in Lecanto, near Ocala, then turned around and went back home because his wife Jo was seriously ill. Our friends Clay and Sally Hart, formerly with the Lawrence Welk Show, came over from Cocoa Beach and Sally, a real champ, stood and sang *How Great Thou Art* a cappella. I was told the church held 1500 and it was nearly full.

The day after losing Perri, I phoned Leroy Kelly in Indian River County, on the other side of the state, to ask a big favor. He's my adopted brother. I said I'd written a lengthy eulogy for Perri but there was absolutely no way I could read it. It would be too emotional for me. I'd never get through it. I asked if he'd come over from Vero Beach and do me the honors. Without pause, he said, "I'll be there brother," and did a remarkable job.

PERRI'S EULOGY: Just a few days ago, on a quiet sunny afternoon, Perri Jo gently went home to be with her Lord. She was surrounded by her loving family and friends. P.J., as she was fondly called, was born in Clearwater on December 6, 1958. She was an early Christmas gift to her mom and dad and grandparents. Parents are always proud and excited about this "gift" God has "given" them. And in a sense, children are precious "gifts." But as my dear friend Bruce Little told me, children are even more than gifts—they are on "loan" from God. In a sense, God is both the owner and loaner of souls. We are entrusted with our children by Him and they are to be cherished, nurtured, and loved. P.J. knew and accepted this premise because she was passionately devoted to her children Olivia, Garrett, and Mariah. She put them first, above all else, body and soul.

In high school, Perri had her moments of hippy liberalism. She played the guitar, sang protest songs, preferred torn jeans, and tie dyed T-shirts. She had her likes and dislikes but I don't recall her ever having fear of anybody or anything even as a child. Perri had a sharp eye for nature and could spot a hawk in a tree a half mile away or a rabbit hiding in the foliage. She would pick up a snake or a critter in the wild. She saw beauty in the simplest of things.

Just out of high school, Perri had her first bout with Hodgkin's disease. At that time medical experts suggested it was generally incurable. Perri took it in stride and whipped the disease by changing her attitude and diet. She ground her own grain, baked her own bread and ate foods that were deemed natural. She maintained a healthy and stable mind by being accepting of all people and loving her Lord.

A few years later, after she married, she had her second fight with the disease, electing to forgo chemo or radiation. She beat it again with a nutritional regimen and her unwavering faith in God. Despite doctors' opinions she had three healthy children and was later described by medical professionals as a walking miracle.

Perri was not distracted by her poor health. She home schooled her kids. Mariah entered high school reading at a college level. All three children have stayed at the top of their classes.

In the grand scheme of things children should outlive their parents. Yet, Perri left us prematurely, much too early—in the blink of an eye she was gone. She was the loving daughter—the good and faithful wife; she fought the good fight—she was a noble and faithful Christian. From the time she was a young mother she wore the mantle of a Christian with great purpose and dignity. She was true to her faith. God expects no more.

Today we celebrate Perri's life. A life, in a way, characterized by the song "Sunrise, Sunset" from Fiddler on the Roof.
"Sunrise, sunset, swiftly go the years . . . one season following another . . . full of happiness and tears." We all have had
our share of happiness and tears as did Perri. By the grace
of God, Perri has passed into the future of hope by trusting
in the grace and love of God. And today, I see my daughter Perri happy to be where she is, looking around, wide
eyed, whispering with wonderment and joy, saying, "Oh,
I've always lived here!"

So, I ask, when you see a mother and a small child laughing, coaxing a home-made kite in the summer sky . . . think
of Perri.

When you see a slow moving storm far out in the Gulf
with low thunder and silent lightning . . . think of my Perri.

When you smell newly cut grass in the gentle rains of
Spring and a brilliant rainbow in the east . . . or a field of
Sunflowers in the morning light . . . think of P.J.

A couple days after losing her mother, Mariah showed me a little
black, blue eyed kitten . . . just four weeks old. Its name is P.J. So,
when you see a baby kitten swatting at a dust ball or chasing a toy
. . . think of my Perri.

There is no greater love than that of a father for his daughter. And
if I may share a bit of advice to the mothers and fathers here today,
that guidance would be to love your children as much as you can,
while you can. One never knows when God may call-in His loan.

I close with a verse by Tennyson, my Grandfather's and my Dad's
and my favorite poet:

Sunset and evening star . . . and one clear call for me.

*And may there be no moaning of the bar . . . when I put
out to sea.*

For tho' from out our borne of Time and Place.

The Flood may bear me far . . . I am with my Pilot, face to face

For I have crossed the bar.

"May flights of angels sing thee to thy rest"

I've learned that sometimes, life can seem like a long and harried highway. Negatives and positives banging into each other like atoms inside a lead basketball. We muddle along, and in the dark hours we metaphorically hit stretches of loose gravel churning up dust, hitting potholes, hearing puzzling noises. Vision is limited. Still we keep both hands on the wheel and press on.

Figuratively, I advocate pulling into a rest stop every so often to check on directions, and perhaps give somebody a lift or a handout. With introspection, life can be a sunny mountain parkway, above the clouds with unencumbered scenic overviews. At those heights earth is a little more defined and we can, more often than not, see the face of God. Since my dad's passing I've learned to accept life as a journey. That's how I've coped with the loss of loved ones: my grandfathers, Marilyn, my dad, my mother, my close friends, and then Perri. It has become easier to believe that this life is simply a fragment of a long and meaningful voyage of the soul.

Have I reached inner peace? No, not totally. But thanks to Brenda, my wife, I'm a lot closer to it spiritually today than I was four or five years ago. I suppose it takes some of us longer than others to see that far horizon. I'll not lecture how precious life is. If you don't know, you'll find out before the fat lady sings. If you're lucky (like me) you'll be given the time to learn, find out. It's only natural in the scheme of things that we should become wiser as we age. Some don't, I'll give you that.

My dad, like his dad, was an unpretentious carpenter and, I believe, an old soul. I rarely heard him wish for stuff. Oh, he always wanted a Cadillac. He never got it. I thought if I ever hit it big I'd buy him a new one. It didn't happen. But with age comes wisdom, or should, and most of us stop wishing for tangibles and consciously take inventory. We begin to appreciate the value of health, family, friends, and precious memories.

Stashed under my bed is a 1942 Gibson guitar that Dad bought new for $50. The instrument remains in mint condition and it'll never be sold in my lifetime. When I was three years old, I waddled over as he played his new J-45 and dropped a spiny cocklebur— about the size of a large grape—into the sound hole. Dad didn't bother removing it and the burr rattled around in the guitar for 10 – 20 years. He never complained or explained why he left it in there for so long . . . or what notion caused him to remove it. Every so often I pull out that old six-string, wipe it down and play a few chords. Likewise, in my closet is a .22 single shot J. Stevens rifle. It's old, too. Dad said he was 14 when he traded a hound dog for the gun. When I was 10 or 12, I was allowed to go out alone with the gun, head out across George Borror's pasture, down the hill, cross Bean Creek and make for the timber and hunt squirrels. I have Dad's books, his art work, carved figurines, sketches, and primitive Grandma Moses style paintings. These humble things bring me gentle memories and I'm grateful to have them.

We lost Dad in 2009 and Mom in 2010. They were nearly 94 years in age and had long and meaningful lives. I miss and think of them every day.

Above my bed, on a glass shelf next to some of my favorite books is a small wooden music box that belonged to my mother. I have no idea how she came to possess it. It's about 3 ½ by 4 inches in size, and resembles an early 20ᵗʰ century pump organ. At its back one winds a silver key to listen to a few bars of the tune *Memories*.

In 2011, we lost Perri, my oldest daughter.

Then, not long ago, while shuffling through a cardboard box of old photographs, looking for pictures for this book, I came across an old postcard from Perri. On one side was a color sketch of a shy eyed little boy, outfitted in an artist's gear, holding a picture frame in front of a flower. It said *To God be the Glory!* With the card, Perri thanked me for a diminutive Beatrix Potter spoon I had sent her from Myrtle Beach. At the time, she and Jim were living in Ft.

Myers and she was fighting another bout with cancer. She wrote, *Hi Dad! I received my rabbit spoon today. Cute! I love it and I'm going to sign up for the rest of the collection. I better read Potter's stories so I can get acquainted with the characters. She thanked me again and signed, with love PJ.*

The card is a small and precious possession I will treasure forever.

LOSS OF A LOVED ONE: The reality of it all is that you will grieve forever. You will not 'get over' the loss of a loved one; you will learn to live with it. You will heal and you will rebuild yourself around the loss you have suffered. You will be whole again but, you will never be the same. Nor should you be the same, nor would you want to.

Elizabeth Kubler-Ross & John Kessler

CHAPTER EIGHTEEN

The Song Writer

MANY SONGS I'VE WRITTEN were about observations and experiences that I had when I was in law enforcement. Some were not so funny, and some were funny. I was hanging with the guys one night, shootin' the breeze after the 3-to-11 shift, and was challenged by Frank Holloway to write a song about our profession. He pointed out that besides the hazards of just being cops we patrolled in high powered automobiles that were not equipped with seat belts or air conditioning. Holloway rationalized, where else does an employer hand you a gun and expect you to drive a car at blistering speeds without a seat belt, chasing drunk drivers, bad guys, bank robbers, and signal-20s (the mentally disturbed)? He said, "The FAA requires seat belts in airplanes. They put seat belts in race cars but cops don't get the same consideration. What's with that?"

When I first went with the sheriff's department, our cruisers had centrifugal sirens under the hood that ran off the engine's fan belt. It's funny now, but when you were running *10–18!*, driving fast with red light and siren on, trying to get someplace in a hurry or chasing someone, you had to push the horn ring on the steering wheel to activate the siren—but that caused the car to slow down! No kidding. It was a Catch-22 situation. If you wanted to catch the bad guy you had to lay off the siren.

I'm reminded of what my buddy General Sandy Sharpe (Retired) told me about flying the A-10 Thunderbolt II in the first Iraqi War. He said the jet, called the Warthog, is built around a massive 30

mm Gatling autocannon designed specifically to knock out tanks, and when it's fired the plane actually slows down.

Sandy told me he destroyed thirteen Soviet made T-72 tanks. I asked him how many people he killed. He said, "I didn't kill anybody, Sheriff. We'd fly in low over our targets, and the Iraqi tank crews would bail out and we'd come back around and turn Saddam Hussein's armored equipment into heaps of melted and mangled steel."

I penned *Hey There Fuzz*, a tacky little ditty enjoyed by the squad during fried mullet and hushpuppy feasts. Incidentally, when I recorded this song in Nashville, guitarist/session leader Jack Eubanks laid down a primo acoustic guitar track that elevated my shabby little tune to "dang, that's some kind'a real good!"

HEY THERE FUZZ

Well, he works alone beside the gun

All alone beside that gun

All through the night

In the pale moonlight

Working alone beside that gun

Hey There Fuzz with your bright shinin' star

Chrome .38 and those air conditioned cars

Good guys and bad guy

Rifles and riots—three K meetings

And those barroom fights.

Well, the juke box's loud but can't be heard

The noise is from the 53 [avenue tavern]

The bright lights are on

A fight don't last too long

Smell from a stink that's just been stirred.

Hey There Fuzz with your bright shinin' star

Chrome .38 and those air conditioned cars

Good guys and bad guy

Rifles and riots—three K meetings

And those barroom fights.

A bar—a fight—a broken head

And all for something some drunk said

A busted mouth is free

Black eyes that barely see

And all for something some drunk said

Hey There Fuzz with your bright shinin' star

Chrome .38 and those air conditioned cars

Good guys and bad guy

Rifles and riots—three K meetings

And those barroom fights.

THE GATOR BAR: Once upon a time in Largo, there was a honky-tonk bar in the downtown arcade. The place was a favorite hangout for the conservative blue collar worker, the truck driver, the auto mechanic, the citrus worker, the roofer, you name it. I liked saying that the *Gator Bar* was the kind of place—on a Friday or Saturday night—where they'd pat you down to see whether or not you were carrying a gun. If you didn't have one, they'd give you one.

In the 50s and 60s, Largo was considered by some to be the red-neck hub of Pinellas County. Today, it is respectable, and the third largest city in the county. Centrally located, it is the crossroads of the county. As of the last census, the city had a population of 77,648 and boasts a Cultural Center. I'd call that an oxymoron.

There is a tale about a woman who walked into the *Gator Bar* late one night, and after a few beers, she told the bartender the sad story that she'd been married three times, and was still a virgin. The barkeep said he found that difficult to understand or believe. With a tear in her eye she said it was true. Her first husband was a midget, he couldn't reach it. The second husband was a priest and he wouldn't touch it. Her third husband was a Largo cop . . . he couldn't find it.

I fashioned *Gator Bar* after an old joke, told and retold around pubs and juke joints. The story dealt with a peculiar little guy that few people knew much about. I named him Billy Cole. He was a devious little cat who kept to himself and had many misdeeds credited to him. When backing up Largo officers, answering disturbance calls at the *Gator Bar*, I'd see Billy Cole, who appeared to be chatting, not to anyone in particular, but to himself.

Stay with me on this. The last line of the old joke went like this, "... when he wakes up, tell him that was a tire iron from a '65 Ford." So, for the song, I changed the ending to the following single spoken line, "If and when that cat wakes up, tell 'im that was a crowbar from Montgomery Wards."

GATOR BAR

Billy Cole was a small man . . . and he drank at the Gator Bar

His pleasure was mindin' his own business and sippin' from a Mason jar

All his habits were a mystery . . . but everyone seemed to know

When 9 P.M. rolled around the Gator Bar would see Billy Cole.

One Saturday night—after dark—this dude and his chick walked in

Now the guy was big and he had a big mouth—he wanted to impress his friends

*So he strolled the bar and singled out Billy and struck him
from behind*

*The small man folded and fell to the floor—stilled with an
achin' mind.*

*The big man grinned and yelled at the crowd as he pretended to
wipe off his hands: "Tell that boy when he wakes up, that was judo
from Japan!"*

*A short time later Billy Cole came-to and he climbed to the top of
his stool*

*He knew about judo and karate from Korea but his momma didn't
raise no fool*

*So he stepped outside and soon returned, walked over to the giant
in the booth*

*The big man cringed then crumpled up—it was big mouth's moment
of truth*

Billy Cole walked out the door to the strains of the juke box chords,

[Last lines to be spoken]

*And he said, "If and when that cat wakes up . . . tell him that was
crowbar from Montgomery Ward's."*

KOOL AID TATTOO: The idea for this song came to me when I
was a uniform deputy. Once in a while, the S.O. would get a call
from a frantic parent, reporting that their youngster was missing.
A child's safety, of course, was always uppermost in everyone mind
and so a deputy would be quickly dispatched to assess the situation, get a description of the kid, what he was wearing, his habits.
If the circumstances appeared serious more deputies were brought
in, neighborhood search groups were organized and a hunt conducted. Fortunately, during my time, there was never a child that
came to harm.

On the other hand, after I had been on the job a while, and had a little experience, I would breakout the flashlight and do a thorough search of the house. More often than not, the little booger had crawled into a hidey-hole with a toy or puppy and drifted off to sleep. I know, because it happened at our house.

When performing *Kool Aid Tattoo,* I introduced the song by telling about the time Scott came up missing. He was about 3 – 4 years old and after a frantic search we found him asleep in the closet behind his toy box. Scott drank Kool Aid from sunup to sundown, and at the end of the day he had a mustache across his upper lip that steel wool wouldn't take off. One afternoon, I heard this unsettling noise out in the kitchen. Scott was scrubbing down some toads in the kitchen sink. We were the only people in town that had a bunch of albino toads with bloodshot eyes in our yard.

KOOL AID TATTOO*

One summer evening about suppertime

A mamma called for help—her child she couldn't find

Dad began to search—the other kids were scared

A little boy was missing and a neighborhood cared

BRIDGE: *Has anybody seen any little blue shoes*

On a small dirty boy with the KOOL-AID TATTOO

He's followed by a puppy—that's partly wild

His front teeth are missing . . . not the dog's but the child's.

A drummer and a soldier—he played over there

At the edge of the trees—where the grass is bare

He gathered field flowers and different colored rocks

And other secret things that he hid in a box.

He once had a rooster and a bug on a thread

And for weeks he kept a grass snake—even though it was dead.

He once scrubbed some toads in the kitchen sink

They came out very clean but their eyes had turned pink.

BRIDGE: *Has anybody seen any little blue shoes*

On a small dirty boy with the KOOL-AID TATTOO

He's followed by a puppy—that's partly wild

His front teeth are missing . . . not the dog's but the child's.

And then he was found curled up like a fox

Asleep in the closet behind his toy box

Then everyone saw those little blue shoes

On a small sleepy boy—with the KOOL-AID TATTOO.

*Audio available for this song at http://www.darylmaycomedy.com/#!audio/
vstc3=music

PAYDAY'S CHILD

The Harmony Bar was a juke-joint near the corner of US-19 and East Bay Drive. The back parking lot was adjacent to the TriCity Diner. The place has been gone a long time. Incidentally, a similar watering hole called Troy's Lounge was further to the west, closer to Largo's city limits. Surprisingly, Troy's wife's name was Helen and by redneck standards was "a real looker." Her face was said to have launched a thousand fights.

The Harmony Bar was a favorite hangout for Largonians "from the other side of the tracks." They were mostly skilled white laborers with limited education. They poured cement and hauled citrus and livestock. They worked in construction or labored in the sun in the orange and grapefruit groves. Some eked out livelihoods netting mullet or running crab traps or operating tiny fish camps around the shores of Old Tampa Bay.

Proud, productive, and patriotic, they worked hard and hoped for better lives. Some traced their lineage back beyond the War for

Southern Independence. They would say with a measure of levity, "The Civil War ain't over with yet. Us southerners are just settin' around waiting for supplies."

They went to the Harmony Bar to participate in communal fellowship and to consume generous quantities of alcoholic refreshment. They shot a little eight-ball, blew fists-full of quarters on honky-tonk country music, the likes of Faron Young's *Hello Walls,* and Webb Pierce's plaintive whiner *There Stands The Glass.* Beef jerky was plentiful and there were green crocks of boiled eggs and pickled pig knuckles marinating in brine setting along the bar top. Popcorn and unshelled peanuts were considered finger foods.

Despite the bar's reputation, there were few complaints or disturbances. Maybe that was because of the joint's proximity to the sheriff's office. The unpainted cinder block building had a wooden bar that extended the full length of the inside east wall. The remaining space was cluttered with metal and wooden tables, and mismatched straight back chairs. The uneven wood floor, oily with crushed peanut hulls, was worn and saturated with years of spilled beer and Mad Dog. Dotting the floor were tin can lids nailed over knot holes to shut out rats and other vermin. A sign above the bar warned patrons against entering the place unshod.

The joint smelled intensely of cigarette smoke, stale brew, and cheap wine.

But, I digress. During the evening shift, it was easy to circle the *Harmony Bar* at the start of the shift. Before heading in to gas up at the end of the night, I'd drive through the rutted gravel parking lot.

One Friday afternoon, at the beginning of my shift, I spotted a small boy nonchalantly hanging out a window of a fairly new four-door Chevy parked at the back door of the Harmony Bar. He was drinking a bottle of Coke and gnawing on a grubby fist full of pretzels. I surmised a parent had slipped inside for cigarettes or a quick six pack and would soon return. After all, what parent would mindlessly leave a child unattended for a long period of time? We made eye contact. He seemed to have participated in this drill before.

"There's a grubby little boy with cold dirty hands, he plays outside of the bar . . ."

I moved on down US-19 towards St. Petersburg's Haines Road where the hunting was better on weekends.

Around ten-thirty, when ending my shift, I returned to circle the *Harmony Bar* and spotted the same little guy playing in the dirt. The vehicle had not moved. The hood was cold. As I walked over, he eyed me warily. This was not his first encounter with a lawman. I smiled, and asked about his parents. He pointed and said, "My mom's in there."

I asked, "Where's your daddy?"

The little man-child said, "My dad's workin' in Jacksonville."

The new car's seats were littered with pop bottles, candy wrappers, and empty chip bags.

I entered the bar with nightstick in hand. The night was going fast and the noisy, whooping patrons were drowning out Waylon Jennings on the juke box. I whacked the bar heavily with my nylon baton and got the undivided attention of all attendees. With inflated authority I looked at Jack, the bartender, and asked who was responsible for "that kid out there in the parking lot?"

A well-dressed young woman at a back table jumped up and scurried to my side. She was in the company of a guy that had all the looks of a sleazy used car salesman. She confessed in low tones that the child was hers, saying she'd only stopped off for a beer but time had gotten away. She begged me not to take the issue further, saying she was not in the habit of doing such shameful things. She feared her abusive husband would learn of her extracurricular activities.

"Ain't no tellin' what he'd do to me again," she whined.

I made threats, she made promises. Then she went to the table, collected her belongings, passed a slow hand across the hustler's chest and darted out the back door like a hummingbird. I wrote this song:

PAYDAY'S CHILD*

[C.1963-64]:

There's a grubby little boy with cold dirty hands, he plays outside of the bar

It's now ten o'clock and he's been there since four, in a parking lot filled with cars

He comes with mom and they meet the old man when it's payday at the mine

Mom and dad go inside and the little guy tries to find something to pass the time.

He's Payday's Child, payday's neglect,

It happens every weekend

It's been that way every Friday,

And loneliness . . . has become his friend.

A bunch of beer cans lined up on a log; in the dirt he draws a line

Hitches up his pants then throws the rock and knocks 'em off one at a time

Dirty wood floors smell of old spilled wine and a neon glares through a pane

Outside in that light is a child of the night, he's standing there in the rain.

He's Payday's Child, payday's neglect,

It happens every weekend

It's been that way every Friday,

And loneliness . . . has become his friend.

Midnight come 'round and he's hard to be found anywhere near or far

He's been given some candy and had a coke and left to sleep in the car

*He fears the law 'cause they haul off his pa sometimes when the
fightin' goes on*

*He'll run and hide till mom comes outside and she'll take him home
all alone.*

He's Payday's Child, payday's neglect,

It happens every weekend

It's been that way every Friday,

And loneliness . . . has become his friend.

*Audio available for this song at http://www.darylmaycomedy.com/#!audio/
vstc3=music

LOCKWOOD SEEGER was created during my dealings with all
the alley prowlin', card playin' pool sharks and red whisky dealers
around Pinellas County. In the daylight hours, Lockwood operated
a semi-legitimate car repair shop. After dark, his place of business
had all the amenities of a Seven-Eleven, a drive-through liquor
store, a clandestine crap game, a surreptitious dating service and,
because of his enormous liquidity, a flim-flam loan enterprise that
he called "baggin' and bankin'" or "greasin' the greens." Lockwood
was a fearless womanizing and a free-wheeling, money making
machine.

Lockwood joked that he was the original "spote" (sport) and
explained that an authentic "spote" was a dude circumcised with
pinking shears. He said, "It do thrill the ladies."

LOCKWOOD SEEGER

1.] Lockwood Seeger owns a radiator shop,

He got junk all over the place.

His mamma says he works too hard

But he always got a smile on his face.

All the men in town say, "He trouble,"

But the ladies say, "He cool!"
"Cause a mechanic ain't no mechanic
Unless he's handy . . . with his tools."
2.] He's got a ping-pong table in the paint stall
He's got shine in 'frigerator
Crap game every Saturday night -
He'll get all your money sooner or later.
Lockwood Seeger is a radiator man
A mechanic of the first degree
But Lockwood loves his cards and booze
And ladies are his specialty.
3.] Lockwood Seeger cain't read or write
but he sure as hell can figure
When trouble starts in town
you can bet your ass it's Seeger
He got a .44 magnum in his car -
He got a tire iron under his seat
He got a throw down knife up his sleeve -
That's a combination you cain't beat.
4.] Lockwood Seeger play the harmonica -
He drive a brand new car.
He got one gold tooth in his mouth -
And it's made in the shape of a star.
He wears two-tone perforated shoes -
Color black and white
He got one orange tie
And he wears it every night.
(Repeat first verse)

SEVEN MILES FROM NOWHERE

Bill Henson was a Largo cop. He was a big guy, agreeable, handsome, and could finger-pick a flat-top in the style of legendary Merle Travis. He was a look-alike for film actor Forrest Tucker. Bill once told me I sounded like Willie Nelson when I sang. "But," Bill said, "You're better." "Have you ever heard Willie sing *Blackjack County Chain Gang?*" I had not.

Bill presented an arresting figure in uniform—no pun intended. He was fair-minded, but flat out loved to scrap. He also loved sipping whiskey and chasing women. He was adept at all.

Bill found it difficult to take law enforcement seriously and consequently was incorrigible. He would say, "You can always tell a Largo cop, they're the ones that yell at you, 'Pull over there, boy! Now take this here ticket and write what I tell you to.' The department can't afford sirens so they use cats in heat."

He enjoyed telling the story of a man who was informed by his doctor that he only had six weeks to live. The doctor asked the doomed man what he planned to do? He responded, "I'm gonna move to Largo." Asked why, he said, "It'll seem like six years."

One clammy Florida night after finishing our respective shifts, Bill and I ran into each other in the parking lot of the Tri City Diner, on the southwest corner of US-19 and East Bay Drive. I had managed to acquire a measure of sippin' stuff and we proceeded to imbibe in the sheriff's unmarked car. As the night wore on and the bottle emptied Bill told me a long, sad story about Willie Dunn, his childhood buddy in Crandall, Georgia, and that Willie died jumping from a moving freight train. I asked Bill, "Where the heck is Cradall, Georgia?" Without thinking, he responded, "Aw, about seven miles from nowhere." I went home, wrote down some notes and eventually wrote *Seven Miles from Nowhere.*

SEVEN MILES FROM NOWHERE

Walking along that river 'neath that ol' Georgia moon

Thinking about Willie Dunn and the times we'd hunt for 'coon

Thinking about our childhood and the times we use to share

Back in Crandall, Georgia—Seven Miles from Nowhere.

Daddy died of a gunshot and mamma she died sad

Willie Dunn was my buddy, all the family I ever had

We grew up cutting' pulp wood and the bad times they were rare

Back in Crandall, Georgia—Seven Miles from Nowhere.

Willie Dunn was a rebel . . . and the best friend I ever had

We'd clean out a bar in minutes, sometime ol' Willie got real bad

He was always there to guard my back—we sure made a fightin' pair

Back in Crandall, Georgia—Seven Miles from Nowhere.

One night we'd been a drinking, hopped a freight train back to town

The engine started screaming, the railroad bridge was down

I cleared the car in second, Willie tried . . . to step it wide

Hit his head on a cross tie and that's where Willie died

Back in Crandall, Georgia—Seven Miles from Nowhere.

Bill Henson quit Largo P.D. and worked with a couple other police departments before alcohol finally got the best of him. I lost track of my old friend.

After I left, my brother Gary went to work for the Pinellas County Sheriff's Office. He finally got around to telling me a story that was typical Bill Henson.

One afternoon, Gary sat alone in the sheriff's substation in the town of Safety Harbor. The small office was attached to the city's fire station on Main Street. Suddenly the door burst open and a big man, bleary eyed and unsteady, loudly announced he was there to kick a deputy's butt. Gary got up, seized the inebriated soul, placed him against the wall and manacled him with a shiny pair of S&W cuffs. The sullen prisoner was then walked through the station, between the fire trucks, to a green and white cruiser curb-side and placed in the back seat. All the firemen on the afternoon shift, aware of the commotion, idly watched as the sheriff's cruiser pulled out, headed for the county jail in downtown Clearwater.

Once on the highway, Bill Henson became chatty. "What's your name?" he asked through the wire cage.

"Gary May," came the answer from the front seat.

"You know Daryl May?"

"He's my brother," says my brother

"Well, your brother and me wrote a song together . . . *Seven Miles from Nowhere.*"

Gary responded, "Yep, I know who you are, Bill, and I know the song."

After a few miles of reflection, my brother said, "I'll tell you what, Bill, if you can sing *Seven Miles from Nowhere,* all the way through, every verse, I'll take you back to Safety Harbor."

Thereupon, Bill, the prisoner, sang the song in its entirety. With that, my brother Gary made an abrupt U-turn in the middle of busy US-19, drove back to Safety Harbor, and parked in front of the fire station. Bill Henson was gently helped from the back seat, the cuffs removed and he wobbled off down the oak and moss shaded street into oblivion.

Bewildered, the firemen, scratched their bums and inquired, "What the hell was that all about?"

Gary answered, "He's a friend of my brother."

LARGO EIGHT

They weren't the common criminals we see on TV
That run dope rings or commit larceny
They didn't kill for money—they didn't buy votes
They didn't hang around grade schools in long rain coats
No! These trailer park terrors—these over-the-hill mates
Played poker for pennies—The Largo Eight
Sitting around, drinking bourbon and poly grip
Gin and denture cream—Bingo wasn't their bag
Then one afternoon—unarmed and alone
Two Coleman raiders slipped into the Geritol zone
With bullet proof cue sticks their only defense
They bravely shot pool and gathered evidence
The deputies would triumph this $24 dollar game
But little did they know they'd reap national fame
Outnumbered four to one—risking life, tempting fate
They swooped in and busted—The Largo Eight
Well a cry went up all over this land
That mercy should be shown these eight desperate men
But the law is the law—and the jury came in
Guilty as charged for their heinous sin—The Largo Eight
So granny and grandpa if you want to retire
And stay out of the law's line of fire
Just learn to fly an airplane—it's your only hope
"Cause poker's more dangerous than dealing dope.

With the help of Jerry Burr's recording skills and guitar work, and T. C. Jacks blowing a wailing harmonica, I sang and recorded a demo of *A Mean Wind A'Blowin'*. The song was about the ravaging hurricane of 1928, called the Okeechobee Hurricane, also known as San Felipe Segundo Hurricane, and was the second deadliest tropical cyclone in the history of the United States.

The storm made landfall near West Palm Beach, with winds of 145 mph. More than 1,711 homes were destroyed. Yet, Lake Okeechobee and the surrounding area were the hardest hit. Locally referred to as "The Big O", Lake Okeechobee is the second largest freshwater lake contained entirely within the contiguous 48 states. It covers 730 square miles, and is exceptionally shallow for a lake of its size, with an average depth of only nine feet. The storm surge in 1928 caused water to pour out of the southern edge of the lake, flooding hundreds of square miles to depths of twenty feet. At least 2,500 people drowned.

Remember Paul Catoe, the weather guy with Channel 8 News, in the 70s? After doing the six o'clock evening news, Paul would come over every so often to Clearwater with Jack Harris and news anchor Bob Hite to catch my show. They'd have one or two toddies before heading back to Tampa to do the 11 o'clock news. Paul and I became friends. He liked my hurricane song and played it a few times as the theme for the Channel 8 pre-hurricane specials. Paul surprised me one night by showing up with Dr. Neil Frank, head honcho with the National Weather Service (NWS) out of Miami. Frank needed to hear *Mean Wind A'Blowin'*. As a result of that kind gesture, my song was the opening and closing theme for the NWS's pre-hurricane special for a couple years. I'm kind'a proud of that.

A MEAN WIND A'BLOWIN'

There was something in the air—you could feel it everywhere

And the panthers in the Glades began to cry

*It was the hurricane of 28 and the wind sounded like a racing
freight*

And 1,800 souls were about to die

The old timers still remember—it was the middle of September

Lake Okeechobee was blown dry

About 50 years this season—that killer storm for no reason

Screamed out of the South Atlantic and came this way

*There was a death like calm over Mexico and a hot wet wind swept
Orlando*

And the birds had all flown from Tampa Bay

*And in just a few hours all of God's powers brought death and
destruction all around*

*And the dead never made it to high ground—the wind made a
screaming devil sound*

Now there's something in the air—you can feel it everywhere

Mammas grab your babies and cry -

*'Cause there's A Mean Wind A 'Blowin'—there's a bad moon a
glowin'*

There's a high tide runnin' on Tampa Bay

All the palm trees are swayin' and the pine trees are laying'

In the sand . . . and that's where they'll stay

All the high lines are hummin'—theres'a big wind a'comin'

*You can tell by that devil screamin' sound—mammas get your
babies to high ground*

There's a high tide a'risin' all around

She just swept off the coast of Cubapilin' waters on Boca Chica

This time she's a'comin' through our front door

The big cypress swamp is flooded—all the Keys have been gutted

Cape Sabel just ain't there no more

All the critters that are crawling' in the rain that's a'fallin'

*Can tell by the screamin' devil sound—got to get their babies to
high ground*

There's a flood tide a raisin' all around

There was something in the air—you could feel it everywhere

And the panthers in the Glades are startin' to cry

There was something in the air—you could feel it everywhere

*Mammas get your babies and fly—Mammas get your babies
and cry*

Mammas grab your babies and fly

OKEECHOBEE DEAR

*Keepin' doggies in a thousand acre yard—and dodging
diamondbacks ain't all that hard*

*Fixin' fence on a South Florida range—for a cowboy like me that
small change*

*'Waitin' once a month to get my pay—and it's always late by a
couple'a days*

*We need rain bad but it ain't come yet—but for a shotgun like me
that ain't no sweat*

BRIDGE: *But the hardest time for me is after the sun goes down*

*Sittin' in the Gator Bar while the cowboys gather 'round—they
gather 'round*

They come to shoot a little pool and drink a beer

And talk some trash to my Okeechobee Dear.

Well, I saw her first and satisfied she's mine—I'm the one she talks to at closing time.

But her momma says for her to come right home—that's the time of night I'm most alone

I've seen the eagle soar in the Florida sky—and other sights to sooth this cowboy's eyes

But the prettiest thing I've seen around here—is the sight of my Okeechobee Dear

BRIDGE: *And the hardest time for me is after the sun goes down*

Sittin' in the Gator Bar while the cowboys gather 'round—they gather 'round

They come to shoot a little bull and drink a beer

And talk some trash to my Okeechobee Dear.

They come to shoot a little pool and drink a beer

And talk some trash to my Okeechobee Dear.

Isn't it odd how things sometimes work out . . . or don't? For a while, I had an agent in Nashville. He said, "Do y'know, 'Broadway Joe' Namath, the quarterback for the New York Jets? He owns a club in Tuscaloosa, Alabama. I can get you a two-week gig there, it pays good money." Everybody knew who Namath was. Wow, maybe I'd get to meet the guy. He was show biz, as big as Burt Reynolds. I said let's go for it. Straightaway, I was inspired to write *Turn Me Loose in Tuscaloosa,* thinking it would be a great tune to perform at Namath's place. The lyrics seem a little lame by today's standards. The gig didn't materialize, but the song was frequently requested when I worked clubs south of the Mason-Dixon.

TURN ME LOOSE IN TUSCALOOSA

Turn Me Loose in Tuscaloosa; it's my kind of town

And Bonnie's back from Birmingham, she just stepped off the hound

Turn Me Loose in Tuscaloosa with some greenbacks in my jean

Fist high in watermelon—a white shirt starched and clean

Give me a steel string Tennessee flat top box—a thumb pick for pickin' it right

A flatbed Ford pickup truck—enough woman to last the night

Well, the crowbar hotel is empty but it won't be for long

'Cause Saturday night's a big night and Sundays always go wrong

Turn Me Loose In Tuskaloosa, it's my kind of town

And Bonnie's back from Birmingham, she just stepped off the hound

Turn Me Loose In Tuscaloosa—Ah, Turn Me Loose In Tuscaloosa

The desire for sex ...
Always creates some trouble.

—The Dalai Lama, 80

"I NEVER MET A HOOKER I DIDN'T LIKE"

by Daryl May & T.C. Jacks

I've known some lawyers that I've hated, over paid and over rated

And there's nothing they wouldn't do for gold

I've been to doctors when I'm sick and some I wouldn't take a chicken

Even if they only had a common cold.

Politicians make me shake and CPAs make mistakes

Any anytime you need a cab they're out on strike.

Out of all the folks I've known, there's one group that stands alone

Cause I Never Met a Hooker I didn't Like.

Well now there are folks in all professions who can stimulate depressions

'Til you wish you hadn't even learned the word

From garages to massages they bombard you with barrages

Of the weirdest sounding crap you've ever heard.

Aw this world is full of ringers and I'm sure that you've hear singers

That should never stand before a mike

The only ones who get it right are the ladies of the night

Oh I Never Met A Hooker I didn't Like

FINISH: *Well I think we should acknowledge all those dedicated girls*

Who are out there working in the oldest business in the world

They got their act together and they couldn't do it better

Oh, I Never Met A Hooker I Didn't Like

'Course we don't know what will happen yet tonight.

Up Yours*

BACK BEFORE TELEVISION SETS had hand held remotes there was a back-woodsy kind'a guy selling tires on local TV. He began his pitch with, "Tires ain't purty (pretty)." And for a while friends and I walked around greeting each other with, "Tires ain't purty."

One of my favorite aphorisms is, "A colonoscopy ain't purty." When you Google *colonoscopy* the next reference that pops up is *Colonel Sanders.* Think about that for a minute. I've had two or three of these procedures and, as I write, I'm trying to conjure up the courage to do it again.

||||||||||||||||||||||||||||||||||||||||||||||||||||||||||||||||||||||||||||
When you Google **colonoscopy** *the next reference that pops up is* **Colonel Sanders.** *Think about that for a minute."*

||||||||||||||||||||||||||||||||||||||||||||||||||||||||||||||||||||||||||||

I will say the exploration process I'm referring to is a lot easier if you know and trust the doctor and his pick of other team players.

In case you're not over fifty, and unfamiliar with a colonoscopy, it is a process that allows a doctor to look at the inner lining of your large intestine (rectum and colon). A thin, flexible tube is used to view the colon which helps to find ulcers, colon polyps, tumors, and other flotsam and jetsam that shouldn't be there.

My first procedure was performed by a little black eyed, dark skinned man from some place on the outskirts of Islamabad. His staff said he always ran late which gave me plenty of time to stress out and contemplate the moment. When he eventually showed up, he snapped on those ominous opaque rubber gloves and, with a heavy accent, said, "Okay, it's time to rock and roll." The phrasing was less Elvis, more bin Laden.

Before the event, I waited for Doctor Singh in a prep room big enough to house Patton's Second Cavalry, saddles, tanks, and all. The place was so big there were warehouse-like echoes. No other patients were around, which wasn't a good sign. It was just me. A group of nurses were gathered around like idle condors, quietly chittering. Learning this was my first colonoscopy, they assured me there was absolutely nothing to worry about. I got counterfeit smiles and light, butterfly pats on the wrist. "It's pretty much routine," they said, all nodding seriously in agreement. In the midst of our tête-à-tête, a mousy little thing, who, up till then had been noticeably subdued, turned to me and with shy, watery eyes said, in a timid little voice, that a colonoscopy was simply a way of *looking up old friends.*

My second time around took place at Clearwater's Morton Plant Hospital. Waiting there in the prep room, flat on my back and buck-necked except for a flimsy mini-gown that barely covered my tailgate, Boris Ovenoff, the anesthesiologist, came by to say hello and chat me up like we were old poker pals. No pun intended. I've always wondered why some medical people stand behind you with clipboards and pens on the end of a beaded chain when they talk to you? Do they know something horrific is about to happen and fear their countenance will give it away? It certainly prohibits eye contact, ruling out identifying the perp if the procedure goes south and the patient becomes a victim.

Why don't they just wear a surgical mask, aluminum aviator shades, and a hoodie and get it over with.

Boris, the needle-and-gas guy, assured me that everything was going to be just fine, that the team was made up of highly trained professionals and doo-dah, doo-dah. Then he says doctor So-And-So (who happened to be my friend), told him I was a former singer. He asked what kind of music I liked. I told him when I was singing professionally it was country music although, like Merle Haggard, I no longer cared for the crossover pop crap coming out of Nashville. Feigning interest, he wanted to know my favorite song. So, to give the impression I was unconcerned with what was about to happen, I flippantly told him my all-time favorites were *Butter Beans* and *Up Against the Wall, You Redneck Mother.* He said he'd never heard of either one. No surprise there, his blank stare was a dead giveaway.

All at once a white jacketed bruiser, right out of *One Flew Over the Cuckoo's Nest,* showed up and tossed me around like a hindquarter of warm beef, flipped me onto a wheelie and zipped me down and around hallways, and into an elevator. He talked over me like I was an inanimate object. Finally, I was maneuvered through metal double doors, big swinging things that looked like the entrance to an IHOP kitchen, where I was greeted by the chief router. We'd known each other for a long time. We read the same books, shared the same politics and jokes and last name. But this day, I was eyeing him like Wild Bill Hickok should have minded Jack McCall.

This was not my first visit to an operating room but it was the first time I'd been wheeled in without being put under—medicated. I was wide awake. So, here I was squinting into glaring overhead lights, butt side down on a cold and narrow stainless steel table while the professionals in the room carried on like it was a tailgate party at a Bucs game. I felt relief. The relaxed ambience had taken the edge off my anxiety.

My friend told me to roll over on my left side. Befuddled, I roll right. He corrected me, "No, the other left side." Then he said, "Give me your paw." I extended an open hand and he slapped the probe in it. He said, "Close your fist." Then he told me to look at the TV screen above my head. "That's what it's going to look like when we do the procedure."

It wasn't going to be pretty, friends. TMI?!

This is the same doctor, when meeting my wife Brenda for the first time at a cocktail party, pointed his thumb in my direction and said, "I've seen this guitar picker with clothes on and I've seen him naked . . . (long grinning pause) . . . clothes are better."

When he removed my gallbladder, the sutures failed to dissolve like they were supposed to. One on my front side got a little red and irritated and I went to see him at his office. He told me to get up on the table, then said, "If this hurts let me know." Bam! There was pain. I howled and I let him know it. He told me, "Wait a minute. Let me get a sharper tool."

When I dropped by again to let him take a look at the healing wound he was accompanied by two smocked interns. I protested, saying I wasn't going to pay all three for the visit. He told me, "Don't worry, they're just here to hold you down."

For a long moment, while the doctor was preoccupied and I was lolling wide-eyed, a dark eyed nurse leaned in close like a midnight harlot and whispered in a soft voice, "Do you know what a colonoscopy is, Mr. May?"

What? What is she asking? Why is she asking me that? Bewildered, I say I am no longer certain. All at once she's Cloris Leachman in a KKK uniform. Does she know some hideous secret? I felt her warm breath on my ear. "A colonoscopy," she uttered, "is a length of hose with an asshole at both ends." Snorting, she turned away, pleased with herself. I suspected somewhere in the dark Mel Brooks was filming. It was too late! There was absolutely no way to escape. I was beyond the point of no return. I felt like a tadpole in a coal bucket.

The anesthesiologist stepped up, "I know what, Mr. May," he said, faking spontaneity, "how about you singing a couple lines of *Up Against the Wall, You Redneck Mother?*"

"If it's all the same to you, doc," I tell him, "I'll count like every-body else. One. Twooo. Threeeee . . ." And that's the last thing I remembered.

This time, coming out of anesthesia, six years after my last colo-noscopy, I sensed movement, being shuttled back to recovery. The procedure was inconsequential, I guess, and seemed to have taken only a few minutes.

Faintly cognizant, I continued floating aimlessly on the periphery of La-La Land. Lots of folks were talking, gliding by, smiling. Whee! One nurse reminded me of an actress in the movie *The Sound of Music*. Was it her face, her demeanor, the uniform? She told me loud enough for all to hear that the doctor had pumped air into my colon to facilitate the procedure. Wasn't that sweet, Julie Andrews was telling me in a kindly tone that it was okay to break wind. "Just go ahead," she said, "We don't want you to be uncomfortable or embarrassed."

It was all right, rip off as many as I wanted . . . kind of like "Aint" Bea telling Andy to have all the biscuits and jam he wanted.

From somewhere a voice asked how I'm feeling. I answered, "Great!" and—wow!—I was startled by the clarity of my deep bari-tone voice. Did someone mention John Wayne? Or did I imagine that someone mentioned John Wayne? No matter, I do my best John Wayne when my voice is deep. Inspired, and for no one in particular, I felt obliged to do the Duke: *"If I tell you . . . that a rooster can pull a freight train . . . well, then, you just better hook it up . . . Pilgrim."* That was pretty good. Next, I felt compelled to do my other John Wayne: *"Life ain't easy . . . it's even tougher . . . when you're stupid."*

I would have done Elvis but . . . never mind.

I tried to focus when Brian, the recovery nurse, read a list of things I shouldn't try to do that day. I mustn't drive a car or use power tools. How about an electric tooth brush? Dang, that's soooo funny. I laughed. He smiled. I heard snickers. Whee, again! I was still Peter Pan hovering in a backless gown with my butt hanging out. I probably needed to hush up.

Pete, my doctor, came in, leaned on the bed rail to check on me. "How ya doing?" he asked. "What 'cha drinking," I asked. He said coffee. "Want a cup?" Sure. Then, I heard myself ask, "Hey Pete, have you ever heard *Long Tall Texan* by Henry Strzelecki?" I got an "Oh sure" look that also said maybe I should take a nap. But, I was on a roll, "Hell, nobody remembers that song, it was written in 1959." I couldn't help myself, and started singing it *anyway*, "Well, I'm a long tall Texan; I ride a big white horse ...."

Woo-hoo! Blast me back to oblivion, Scotty!

ONE WEEK LATER I received a hospital operative/procedure report in the mail. It listed details of pre-procedure diagnoses, post-procedure diagnoses, procedure, and final diagnoses. What caught my attention was an inclusion in the procedure narrative. It said; *(The) patient tolerated the (colonoscopy) well. At the end of the procedure, he was chatty.*

Why not witty?

POST SCRIPT: At 6:30 A.M., the day of the procedure, I was admitted into Morton Plant and on my way home by nine. I cannot say enough good things about Morton Plant Hospital. My three kids were born there. It's where my first wife, Marilyn, lost her long struggle with cancer. It's where most of my five grandkids were born and Brenda and I have been in and out of the place a few times for one insignificant reason or another. During all those visits I cannot ever recall the staff being unprofessional or unpleasant.

As for my friend Doctor Farnsworth "Pete" May, well, he's one of my all-time three favorites: the late and dear Paul Straub and Mark Smitherman. Pete and I are still swapping stories, sharing books, talking politics, exchanging jokes, and occasionally lunching at E&E's.

*Thanks to Sally Parks for suggesting Up Yours as the title for this chapter.

ADDENDUM

August 7, 1969: 23:00 hrs. Detective James McAllister filed the following report:

EVIDENCE: Gun: Writer received instruction from Captain Carl McMullen to proceed to the intersection of SR-590 and US-19 and conduct an investigation involving the shooting death of Jack Travis, white male, 35 years old. Writer arrived at the above location and observed (late model) Pontiac, color white, Alabama registration 11-30833, that had come to rest at the bottom of a ditch just south of SR 590 on the west side of US-19 and across from Big Johns Tavern and A.B.C. liquor store. Writer also observed a 1966 Ford 4-door, Florida registration 4-17382 that had come to rest at the edge of the ditch, at a 30 degree angle from the road, and was behind and to the left of the Pontiac. Writer also observed a white male lying on his back in the ditch, behind and to the west of the Ford. Writer and Captain McMullen examined the body and observed what looked to be a puncture type wound in the left chest center. Writer was instructed by Captain McMullen to proceed to the Central Identification Bureau, Clearwater and interview and take statements from several persons there for that purpose.

Writer and Detective Wilson arrived at the records bureau and took statements from the following persons: Ruby Jean Travis, Bernard F., Frances B., Veronica V., and Katherine J. After the statements were given, Gil Thivener, Investigator for the State Attorney's Office, advised that Dick Mensh would be arriving with a court reporter to take statements. Writer advised investigator Thivener that writer was going to take statements from the witnesses but would ask no questions after the witnesses had made their statements. Writer took the statements at this time. When Attorney Mensh arrived with a court reporter, writer escorted all witnesses to the State Attorney's Office, at which time, the witnesses were placed under oath and the statements were taken by the court reporter. Writer received permission to obtain copies of the witnesses' statement from the Court Reporter.

Writer requested Detective Carl Wilson to obtain the name of a close friend of Jack Travis in order to positively identify the body. Writer requested of Deputy Mike Sharpe to take fingerprints and photograph the body and take charge of any projectiles found by Doctor Norton. It was also requested that a blood sample be obtained from the body for test for alcohol content. Writer also requested that fingerprints be taken of the body. Deputies Herb Weller and John Seabach were at the intersection of SR-590 and US-19 and took photos of the scene. Deputy Sharpe advised writer that Dr. Norton performed an autopsy and recovered one projectile and a blood sample was taken. Deputy Sharpe called writer and advised he compared the known prints with the rolled prints and advised that they were the prints of (Jack Travis).

The body was taken from the scene by Lee Ambulance to Moss Funeral Home on the North Ft. Harrison, Clearwater. Writer requested of Deputy Sharpe to search records for complaints on Jack Travis. He advised he had found several records and would copy and send to writer. Writer requested a copy of the traffic accident report by the Florida Highway Patrol and they advised a copy would be sent as soon as it was turned in by the investigating trooper.

At the formal investigation it was learned that the dead man had arrived at Pelican Restaurant and had caused a scene with his wife and at approximately 20:45 hrs. they arrived at The Den and there had been a scene between the dead man and his wife. They were also at the Turf Bar, Oldsmar, where at one time there had been a fight between the dead man and another man. At the above altercations mentioned are to be investigated by this writer and Investigator Gil Thivener on August 8, 1969.

Deputy Seabach called writer and advised that he had taken the keys to the dead man's car and a red waitress's apron that was on the front seat. He also reported that the interior of the automobile smelled like a brewery.

Detective Carl Wilson's report: While working surveillance of robbery suspects in the area of 49th street and 48th Avenue North, between the hours of 23:00 and 23:30 hrs writer heard a call on the Sheriff's radio from Car #89—Detective Daryl May—requesting that a uniform car be dispatched to the meet him at SR-580 and US-19. Deputy Mike Petruccelli arrived at the scene and announced after being directed to do so that Deputy May had shot a subject. Writer and Detective McAllister proceeded to the scene by orders of Captain Carl McMullen who ordered writer and Detective McAllister to go to the SAB and take statements from the witnesses. Upon arrival assisted Mrs. Patricia Lanier and Mrs. Margaret E. Coleman.

Writer then went to 1010 Wyatt Street and asked Mr. James R. Hoffmeyer if he knew Jack Travis and Mr. and Mrs. Hoffmeyer stated that they did know the subject. Writer asked them to identify the body which they did. Mr. Hoffmeyer stated that he had known the subject for twenty years.

Uniform Deputy William H. Bowles Jr. filed the following report: Writer responded to a call for assistance from Deputy Daryl May at approximately 23:21 hrs at the location of SR-590 and US-19. Writer arrived at 23:37 hrs and observed the two vehicles involved sitting in a ditch along the roadside some distance apart from one another. Writer observed a body lying in the ditch on his back with F.H.P. Trooper Ron Gambriel #773, attempted mouth-to-mouth resuscitation on the subject. Writer observed the subject lying in the ditch was not responding to Trooper Gambriel's attempts. Viewing the body at a closer distance, writer observed a wound on the left-center area of the chest. A cloth or dressing was being applied to stop the bleeding.

Lt. Jerry Coleman arrived and took charge of the scene immediately. Writer for the duration of the time worked traffic and kept the scene clear of sightseers.

While at the Sheriff Administration Building writer was told by the victim's wife that her husband was drunk this night and stated that it usually takes three (3) good men to subdue her husband when he gets in this condition.

On 07/17/1966 writer arrested the victim, Jack Travis for attempting to elude a police officer. This occurred during the late evening hours when writer observed a white T-Bird speeding north on Belcher Road. Writer observed a second auto driving recklessly in pursuit of the T-Bird and after using red light and siren writer finally stopped the second vehicle (white Pontiac) at the corner of Belcher Road and Palmetto Street. The driver of the vehicle was Jack Travis. He had been drinking at the time. It was also learned that he had busted up the Wine Cellar minutes before this wild chase. The driver of the T-Bird was Mrs. Pearl Travis who later came down to the scene of the accident and advised that she was being chased by her husband and that she was actually attempting to get away from him fearing for her safety at that time.

Detective Jim Collins filed the following report: At approx. 01:00 hrs writer was called at home by midnight shift Sgt. Jim Brown. Writer was advised of the shooting incident and advised that on Captain Carl McMullen's instructions, I was to proceed to Moss Funeral Home, Ft. Harrison Chapel.

Upon arriving at Moss, writer observed the victim lying on a porcelain table in the preparation room, clad only in a blue pullover shirt. There were visible puncture wounds; one on the right side and one in the chest area. Upon closer examination, a puncture wound was observed on the right buttocks area. Examining the victim's trousers, which had been removed, a hole was observed in the right rear pocket area which appeared to be the exit point, due to the fibers protruding outward.

The victim's physical description is 5' 9", 180–195 lbs., 35 years of age, and muscular.

The autopsy began at 02:09 hrs, by Dr. James O. Norton. First to be examined was the wound on the right waist, which had extremely heavy powder burns. This being the entrance point, with the projectile taking a downward path, just under the skin, glancing off the hipbone area and exiting through the cheek of the right buttocks. The second wound entering between the third and fourth rib, one inch above a one inch medial of left nipple. The projectile passed through the lower portion of the left upper lobe of the lung; entered the left upper chamber of the heart, passed through the aorta into and through the middle lobe of the right lung, then through the fifth rib in a posterior axillary line into the lower portion of the right shoulder blade, lodging beneath the surface of the skin.

The wound entering between the third and fourth rib showed indications that the weapon was held tightly against the victim for the entrance would was large and irregular which would be caused by the exploding effect and also the fact that there were no powder burns on the outside of the skin and that they were in the wound and on the underside of the skin.

80th birthday card to Daryl May from granddaughter Carly Rose May (14)

You are an inspiration, Grandpa.
For all you do and all that you are,
you are loved.
Happy Birthday

"Some men are just naturally cool. Some men just naturally stand out ... they have a sense of purpose, a concern for those around them, and a gift for life. You are one of those men, Poppo, and with every birthday you are loved more and more. Do what makes you happy. Then do it some more. Happy Birthday"

About the Author

JUST SHY OF NINE YEARS, author Daryl May was a uniform deputy and vice cop with the Pinellas County Sheriff's Office in Clearwater, Florida, and he reasons that the time he spent as a lawman equaled at least two Harvard doctorates. Boasting of being trilingual, he says he speaks Yankee, Southern and Redneck . . . in a pinch. Yet, while still a young man, he discarded his Smith & Wesson six shooter and picked up a Gibson acoustic guitar to launch a successful career in show biz.

He performed standup comedy, wrote and sang his own songs and traveled the world while making his home base on a houseboat, Gypsy Dude, tied up on Clearwater Harbor. Occasionally, he slipped off to play gigs in Australia's Snowy Mountains and perform on cruise ships in the Caribbean. Once he found himself frighteningly alone and under fire in the middle of a military coup at Haiti's Port au Prince Airport. During indiscriminate shooting—and surrounded by crowds of unfriendly Haitians—he was suspiciously questioned by sinister-looking military men with dark glasses carrying automatic rifles and battered Colt .45s semi-automatics strapped to their hips. He didn't realize at the time it was a slow day in that country.

Occasionally doing one-night concerts around the country, May mostly alternated between the SeaWake Inn and Stan Musial's Hilton on Clearwater Beach and the Sheraton Hotel in Myrtle Beach, South Carolina. One writer said, "Perched on a stool with acoustic guitar in the soft lights of a nightclub or spotlighted on the concert stage in front of a crowd of 1000, May's one-liners tickled, rather than jabbed, in an easy stream-of-consciousness presentation. He is the only entertainer that can do one-on-one in a large audience and make the others in the lounge feel they are eaves dropping."

May also authored a historical manuscript for the Smithsonian, created and penned an internationally selling children's book, Rachael's Splendifilus Adventure, with PBS artist Roger Bansemer and wrote a hit song for country artist Mel Tillis called The Gator Bar. And for the 10-part PBS TV series titled America In World War II, The Homefront narrated by Eric Sevaried and Ronald Reagan, Daryl composed and performed songs for the program's soundtrack. Additionally, on the final Homefront show, he sang the nostalgic ballad Among My Souvenirs. As a filmmaker, and with help from his wife Brenda, he created an award winning 50-minute documentary on Florida's amazing St. Johns River. It's called Whisper of the River and focuses on the little known traits of the river's connection to Old Florida, unknown even to locals. Review at: https://www.youtube.com/watch?v=2lUk482wUD4&-feature=youtu.be.

After a fulfilling 20-year career in show biz he became director of a fraud investigations unit for Pinellas County, recovering millions for taxpayers.

Today, author Daryl May is working on his fourth book Cue the Cavalry, and lives in Belleair, Florida, with his wife Brenda.

He says, smiling, "My life has been an exciting journey, so far. Moreover, I've learned one very important lesson: never, ever allow self-appointed soothsayers to tell you that you can't do something. If you have dreams, regardless of age, you can make them all come true. So, go for it!"

Website: http://www.darylmaycomedy.com

YouTube: https://www.youtube.com/user/darymay100

Facebook: https://www.Facebook.com/daryl.may.73

Also Available

Books

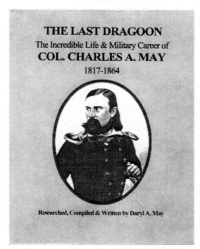

THE LAST DRAGOON
The Incredible Life & Military Career of
COL. CHARLES A. MAY
1817-1864

Researched, Compiled & Written by Daryl A. May

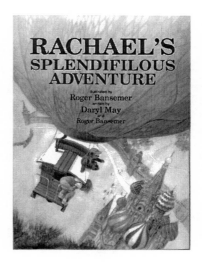

RACHAEL'S SPLENDIFILOUS ADVENTURE
Illustrated by
Roger Bansemer
written by
Daryl May
and
Roger Bansemer

Audio/Video

Daryl May
Comedy Hits
Vol. 1

Whisper of the River
Discover Old Florida's St. Johns River

Available at www.DarylMayComedy.com

CPSIA information can be obtained at www.ICGtesting.com
Printed in the USA
LVOW10s1551190616

493130LV00003B/3/P